THE LIBRARY
OF DEVOTION.

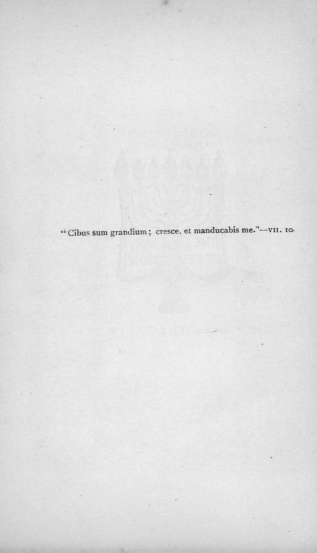

"Cibus sum grandium; cresce, et manducabis me."—VII. 10.

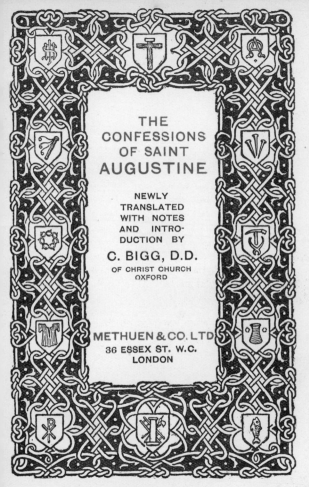

THE
CONFESSIONS
OF SAINT
AUGUSTINE

NEWLY
TRANSLATED
WITH NOTES
AND INTRO-
DUCTION BY

C. BIGG, D.D.
OF CHRIST CHURCH
OXFORD

METHUEN & CO. LTD
36 ESSEX ST. W.C.
LONDON

Ninth Edition

First Published	.	.	March	1897
Second Edition	.	.	December	1898
Third Edition	.	.	December	1900
Fourth Edition	.	.	June	1903
Fifth Edition	.	.	January	1906
Sixth Edition	.	.	October	1907
Seventh Edition	.	.	December	1909
Eighth Edition	.	.	October	1912
Ninth Edition	.	.		1914

CONTENTS

INTRODUCTION

BOOK I

CONTENTS

CONTENTS

BOOK VII

BOOK VIII

BOOK IX

INTRODUCTION

I

Scope of the present Edition.

IT will be observed that the present translation comprises only the First Part of the *Confessions*, that is to say the first nine books. The seventeenth century translations give all thirteen books; the versions issued in the last fifty years include ten books but omit the last three, which contain a Commentary on the first chapter of the Book of Genesis. They were not added by St Augustine without reason, for they contain his view on what may be called the higher criticism of his day, his answer, the best attainable at that time, to some of the difficulties that beset the ever-shifting problem of the relation of science to revelation. But for us the whole ground of this perennial controversy is changed, and this part of the *Confessions* has ceased to have more than a historical interest. It may still be read with profit by those who desire to attain a just view of the system of interpretation which is known as Allegorism. Allegorism was in fact philosophy, and a very fine philosophy, struggling, without

A

the aid of exact science or large historical learning, against the doubts that first suggested themselves to intelligent Christians or to the opponents of the Church. Some of these doubts could be adequately met only by knowledge or by modes of conception as yet undreamed of, and in such cases the Allegorist was often driven to answers which strike the modern reader as forced, or even as absurd. Some of them flowed from those insoluble enigmas which lie at the roots of all thought. In these cases allegorism was the voice of the human reason, as highly cultivated as it has ever been since, and its teaching is of permanent value. Nevertheless it seemed better to exclude the last three books from an edition which is intended for devotional use. The exclusion of the tenth book may be thought more questionable, but there is a natural break at the end of the ninth, the history is completed, the main current of interest ceases to flow, and there seems to be a dramatic fitness in stopping short at that point where the river falls into the lake.

For the purpose of the translation I have used the little text published at Paris by *Jouby et Roger* in 1877. It is rather incorrectly printed, but I have made *sub silentio* such emendations as were needful. In this I have been greatly helped by Dr Pusey's scholarly work. I have kept, for convenience of reference, the received divisions into paragraphs, which are often unskilfully made, and have not altered the headings of the chapters. I have added very few notes, because in a work of this character there should be as little inter-

INTRODUCTION

INTRODUCTION

INTRODUCTION 3

ference as possible between the reader and his
author. What little help is needed will be found,
perhaps, in the later sections of this Introduction.
A few references to Plotinus have been given,
partly because they seem to have been overlooked,
partly because St Augustine was one of the main
channels through which a knowledge of Platonism
trickled down to the earlier Schoolmen and they
have a historical importance on this account,
partly again because they help to modify the stern
view of the saint on the condition of the heathen.
There can be no doubt that the " Books of the
Platonists" translated by Victorinus Afer included the *Enneads* of Plotinus.

Earlier translations that I have seen in the
Bodleian library are the following :—

1. By Sir Tobias Matthew, first edition 1620,
second edition, 1638. The first is anonymous,
the second has a title page written with pen and
ink to replace a lost one. In this the translation
is ascribed to S. T. M. A later hand explains
these initials to mean Sir Tobias Matthews.
There appears to be no doubt that this ascrip-
tion is correct, but the name is generally given as
Matthew.

2. By William Watts, 1631. Watts was
Rector of St Alban's, Wood Street, and wrote
in the hope of drawing off the public attention
from the work of Matthew, which was dedicated
to the Most Glorious Perpetuall and Al-Imma-
culate Virgin Mary, and contained an Introduction
and Notes abounding in controversial matter.
Sir Tobias was a pervert to Romanism, a

priest, and an active proselytiser in fashionable circles.

3. By Dr Pusey, 1838. This forms the first volume of the well-known Library of the Fathers. The title-page has " Revised from a former translation by E. B. P." The former translation was that of Watts, which Dr Pusey used as a basis, but altered and corrected to such an extent that his work was practically new. The remarks made above probably explain why it was impossible for Dr Pusey to follow Matthew, but the work of Watts was more correct, though much less elegant than that of his predecessor.

4. By the Rev. W. H. Hutchings, subwarden of the House of Mercy, Clewer, 1883. There is an earlier edition of this published in 1878 without the author's name.

Dr Pusey's translation is the only one of which I have made any use. I have not scrupled to borrow a few phrases here and there, and the Scripture references given in my pages are in the main taken from Dr Pusey, but with some little amplification. Some readers may think that it would have been better to reprint the version of Sir Tobias Matthew, which has great literary merit, and ought not to be forgotten. But Matthew's flowing Caroline English is for our time archaic. Now St Augustine was for his time essentially a modern man. His easy, plastic style is steeped in literature. Almost every sentence contains some allusion to the Latin Bible, but side by side with these are to be found quotations from the Latin classics, references to the Greek poets, the ideas of the newest Greek philosophy, the artifices of the fashionable Rhetoricians or stylists. All these elements have been fused together in an ardent, poetical, religious imagination, and appear as tints in a style which we may call meditative or devotional, the natural dress of thoughts uttered in the Temple, and not so much heard as overheard. St Augustine's style in the *Confessions* belongs to the same family as that of the *De Imitatione*, the dominant note is the same, but owing to the nature of the subject, and indeed to the nature of the man, it is neither so compact nor so highly polished. St Augustine cannot give the time to cut each word as if it were an individual diamond, as a Kempis did. But there is about both writers the same musical flow, the same spiritual refinement and distinction. This is the great difficulty in the way of the translator, to catch this delicate flavour, which is not exactly to be called exquisite taste, yet bears the same kind of fruit as exquisite taste. Perhaps it cannot be caught, for it depends on hidden qualities of the soul, and is the outward grace of a most beautiful personality. If the reader of the following translation is repelled by any touch of hardness, coarseness, or ostentation, let him throw the blame upon the translator, and rest sure that the starlight of St Augustine has taken alien colours in filtering through the lower air.

II.

Some Prefatory Notes.

THE *Confessions* holds a recognised place, some will think the highest place, on the list of devotional books. It has a character of its own. The *De Imitatione* is the record of a mystic's musings, written in his white-washed cell or among the green meadows of Mount St Agnes, in pleasant pastures, where no noise of archers is to be heard. The *Pensées* of Blaise Pascal are fragmentary notes, the skeleton of an unwritten work on Evidences. What strikes their reader most is the lucid intelligence, the flashing insight, the brilliant logic of their accomplished author. In every sentence there is a sword-thrust delivered with incomparable grace. Law's *Serious Call* is a stern and strenuous summons to reality of life, written in Georgian England by a solid Englishman. A Kempis was an Augustinian canon; Pascal an Augustinian Jansenist. Both were direct spiritual descendants of St Augustine, though the children differed in some very marked features from their father. A Kempis was content to accept theology as the great Schoolmen had shaped it for him, and renounced the strife of words altogether. Pascal was a master of modern science in an age of doubt, and was intellectually an Agnostic. But about both there is the same air of cultivation, the same tendency to soar, the same easiness of flight upwards. Law, on the other hand, in the *Serious Call*, is Arminian and prosaic, and the mysticism which he afterwards adopted came from Behmen ; it is not of the same piece with his Arminianism, nor is it marked by the taste, dignity, and spontaneity of the true Platonic mysticism. But, if Law is inferior to the others in distinction, he has, perhaps, no match in practical force. It is possible to dally with the literary charms of Pascal or à Kempis or Augustine, but few can read the *Serious Call* without great searchings of heart.

From a literary point of view Augustine's book is neither so poetical as the *De Imitatione*, nor so keen as the *Pensées*, nor so practical as the *Serious Call*, though it combines all these qualities in an eminent degree. But its supreme value depends on something very different from artistic excellence. It is a self-revelation. On the one hand it is the record of a moral struggle, a confession, a penitent's confession, which, whatever allowances are to be made for inevitable lapses of memory, is written with absolute truthfulness as in the sight of God. On the other hand it is the authentic disclosure of a rare intelligence, and of the process by which that intelligence lifted itself, or, as St Augustine believed, was lifted up from doubt to certainty.

These two strands, however, are hardly separated in the book, and it is not easy to treat them apart. They are elements of one

life, distinguishable by the reflecting eye, but
springing from a common root and running into
one another, even on the surface, like opalescent
colours. The moral failures act upon the intelligence, and the intelligence reacts upon the
moral failures; they are not really distinct
things. So in the *Confessions* the upward movement of St Augustine's mind is given not merely
as a logical process, not as an argument in form
for the existence of God, such as we may read in
Aquinas or Duns Scotus, but as an effort of the
whole man, thinking at once and climbing, on
feet or knees, or anyhow, wherever he can see
a thread of path. The saint worked out his
problem, not on paper, nor in his study, but by
contact with people and things, by reasoned
intercourse with flesh and blood and the facts
of Nature, by steady questioning of experience
as it came in his way.

It is thus that all men do reach their conclusions on practical questions, especially on
those of the highest import. Theory, by itself,
does not count for much. We want immediately to apply it; it exists only to be
applied. We want to know not merely what
Rousseau or Comte—shall we say?—taught, but
what they did, what they were, what they would
make of us, just as St Augustine, when he had
learned the Manichean doctrines, tested them on
Faustus, on the rank and file of the sect, on
himself. A creed is like an abstract rule of
arithmetic, a rule for ascertaining the unknown
quantities of peace and freedom. We apply it

to one concrete instance after another; if it brings out no answer, or a confused answer, we know that it is wrong. It does not explain the very fact which it undertook to explain, human nature as it exists in living men and women, and, therefore, it stands self-convicted. On the other hand, we know that there is an explanation, and, when we touch it the same test will assure us that we have reached our goal. We shall know that it is true, because the correspondence of theory with fact is what we mean by truth.

This is, in fact, the argument of the *Confessions*. It rests upon Personality; it treats not of abstract human nature but of individuals, of spirits, of living wholes. Hence it does not admit—this must be frankly conceded—of being packed into a logical shape, because logic represents only a part of the man, whereas any tenable theory of life must account for the whole of him.

Hence it is not possible to distinguish really between the moral and the intellectual struggles depicted in the *Confessions*. They differ only as actions of the same will, energies of the same spirit. They are coincident. Augustine did not attain first to self-control and then to truth, nor first to truth and then to self-control, but throughout his story light and power went hand in hand. He saw them as different modes of the same force, and both vibrated from the same Sun. If we were to endeavour to tell his story otherwise than as he told it, we should miss the moral. We can only attempt to present the reader with a few notes, which may help him to understand what he is about to see with his own eyes.

In the first place there *was* a moral struggle. This is the great fact of the book. Augustine went down into the very depths and came face to face with the dragon that dwells there, with the facts of the sensual nature in their barbarous simplicity. There are some who appear never to have had this experience, and they find it possible, to their own great loss, to view religion merely as the most interesting of speculative problems. But Augustine could not take this cool scientific view. He was in the torrent, not watching it from the shore. He was an intensely human man, strongly sensuous and keenly intelligent. The whole of his nature was at war. Reason could not control, desire would not obey, and there could be no peace except in submission to a higher law, which should embrace and harmonise both antagonists.

He went through the whole bitter experience of a divided nature at school, at the University, in the streets, in his profession. It is the familiar but generally carefully disguised story of wilfulness and vice, "a stormy youth," as we politely call it, followed by the decent selfishness of the grown man, who knows that he must keep within bounds if he is to get on. And it is noticeable how little external help he received, and how little profit there was even in the help that did reach him. Indeed this is one of the main lessons of the book. Precisely the same circumstances that give birth to our "problem novels"

shaped Monnica, and precisely the same experience
that makes a clever self-seeking barrister produced
Augustine. This was in his eyes the deepest
mystery of life. Why did Monnica hear God's
voice in the angry taunt of a slave-girl? He was
left almost entirely to himself. His mother
could not control him, his friends were inferiors,
Ambrose he scarcely knew except as he saw him
in the pulpit. There was no particular reason of
interest why he should join the church. The
Rhetoric professor stood very much in the position
of the modern biologist. The church admired
his learning, valued his good word, laid itself out
to capture him, but did not interfere with his
promotion. When Augustine came to reflect
upon the singular relation of circumstances to
life, he felt that his course had been shaped by
something more than his own will. Love had
been calling him, drawing him, gradually kind-
ling an answering love in his own wilful heart.
But why in his and not in others? This is the
question that no man can answer. Augustine is
commonly spoken of as a Predestinarian. But
those who read the *Confessions* will see that what
he means by predestination is not the fiat of an
arbitrary will, but the attraction of one personality
for another. Why do we love anybody? Those
who can explain this can solve the problem of
free-will.

In such a nature as St Augustine's the struggle
was necessarily fierce, even to the dividing
asunder of soul and spirit, and there could be no
peace but in absolute submission to the Divine

Will.   The form of this submission was dictated
partly by his own temperament, partly by the
spirit of the age, and it was the age of nascent
monasticism.   Some may feel that there is room
for criticism here, that Augustine's renunciation
involved too great a sacrifice of the claims of
others.   There were ancient rules of the Church,
for instance in the *Canons of Hippolytus,* which
forbade the casting off of those who were wives
in all but name.   Yet Augustine seems to have
known of no such law.   Anyhow this act too is
frankly confessed, and the reader may draw it
within the same saving plea from "times and
seasons," which the saint employs to justify the
lives of the Hebrew patriarchs.

The intellectual side of Augustine's conversion
may be called either a gradual breaking of the
light, or an ordered series of disillusions.   From
first to last his teacher was disappointment; only
when he found one road closed did he try
another.   Here again there rises before us that
mystery of life, which he will never suffer his
readers to forget.   Experience is always the
same—*medio de fonte leporum surgit amari aliquid.*
Why does this gall in the honey make one man
a pessimist, another an epicurean, while a third
concludes that he has fixed his hopes too low and
struggles on upwards in quest of purer joys?

Augustine allows us to see what was the reason
in his own case.   Though he was unbaptised as
a child, and practically an infidel in his youth,
the name of Christ, "drunk in with his mother's
milk (iii. 4)," remained somehow fixed in the

depths of his mind. Thus he was never wholly bankrupt. The Cross was always drawing him, even when he was not aware of it, and, though at first it did not satisfy, it prevented anything else from satisfying. He was always "salted with Christ's salt" (i. 11). He felt also that the secret of this disquieting power of the Cross lay in its Humility, a grace most alien to his passionate temperament. He tells us again that through all his aberrations he never really doubted that there is a God who punishes evil. If so again the chief of all sins must be pride. How often does he quote the verse "God resisteth the proud." But it was long before he came to understand the full meaning of this confused belief. Through this mist lay the upward road, but he was not likely to try so unpromising a path till all others had failed him.

It was in his nineteenth year that Augustine experienced his first disillusion, and the blow reached him from a most surprising and unexpected quarter. He was leading a vicious life, a close ally of the "fast set" as we should call them—"the wreckers" they called themselves—at Carthage, yet at the same time studying with great eagerness for the profession on which his hopes, and his parent's hopes, were centred. It is not an unfamiliar picture, poor and brilliant youth halting between ambition and luxury. He might have ended in the usual way, by taking ambition for his mistress, for he was a Rhetorician with good prospect of advancement to a professorship in one of the large towns, and possibly to high employment in the Civil Service. But at this juncture he read the *Hortensius*, a treatise now lost except for a few fragments, in which Cicero sang the praises of "divine philosophy." From this moment rhetoric, the art of style, at that time of bombastic Byzantine style, the art of persuasion, of "making the worse reason appear the better," the dangerous art which its unhappy professors must sell to all comers, whatever use they propose to make of the purchase, lost its charms in Augustine's eyes. "This book," he says, "altered my disposition and changed my purposes and desires. . . . Not to sharpen my tongue did I pore over that book." Thus Cicero, the prince of rhetoricians, weaned Augustine from the love of rhetoric.

This was strange, but the mode in which the next step of his progress was brought about seems far stranger. From the day when he unrolled the *Hortensius* Augustine looked upon wisdom as the supreme goal of human endeavour. Where then should Wisdom be found, but in the word of God? This was the fountain, as his mother and the whole Christian world were daily insisting. Augustine turned to the Bible, and turned in vain. He took the revelation in his hand, and, behold, it was a mystery And what made it a mystery was not cloudy grandeur of language, or subtle nicety of thought, but meanness of style and moral inconsistency.

Clement also and Origen as well as Augustine were sorely tried by what they thought the vulgarity of the Scripture narrative. Tried by the received

canons of taste, which approved of nothing but
the diluted, the precious, the inflated, the Bible
seemed to them to possess no artistic merit at all,
and this was a great perplexity, because they knew
that wisdom and true art are very nearly allied.
It did not occur to them that their standard was
vicious. They did not see that simplicity,
directness and self-effacement are as important in
art as in morality. They knew that humility is
the supreme grace of life, yet treated it as a
fault in letters, which are the mirror of life.
They came to love the words of the Bible, yet
always apologised for the very quality that made
them lovable. This curious inconsistency is due
partly to the clumsiness of the Latin and Greek
versions, which in many places sadly disguise
the beauty and even the sense of the original,
but mainly to the obstinate leaven of Greco-
Roman vanity. Not till the prerogative of the
ancient classics had been destroyed by the inter-
vention of the dark ages, was it possible for men
to see that no writer of the Imperial age, perhaps
none even of the classical, could have produced
the last chapter of St John's Gospel. Till that
deluge of ignorance had swept over the earth, till
the Christian world had been thrown for a time
entirely on its own resources, art was always regarded with a certain dread as the enemy of the
Faith. Humility ended by producing new and
finer canons of taste, but in the time of Augustine
these were hardly discernible, least of all in the
sphere of literature.

We can understand better the moral difficulties

which Augustine found in the Hebrew Scriptures, for they are still felt by many. The Higher Criticism, except as regards its strictly philological conclusions, is the formulation of doubts that were quite patent to Celsus or Porphyry or the young Augustine. Was the polygamist Jacob a good man? Was Jael right when she slew Sisera, or Samuel when he slew Agag? Is God angry, does He repent, does He stretch out His arm? Everybody has asked these questions, and many like the ancient Gnostics and Manicheans have met them with a vehement denial, making themselves "the measure of all things," judging the long past and eternity itself in the light of the changing present. Augustine came to see that the history of the world is like a sentence, a long and intricate Latin or German sentence. Every clause has a meaning of its own; but the verb, the emphatic word, comes last, clinching together and shedding light back upon the whole. But first it was ordained that he should learn humility, the purpose of sorrow, and the spirit of history in the school of the Manicheans to whom all these things were absolutely unintelligible.

Manicheeism was a recast of the older Gnosticism, and maintained a kind of subterranean existence from the second century after Christ to the days of Aquinas. During all this time, for more than a thousand years, no man of eminence found it capable of defence, yet multitudes must have made great sacrifices on its behalf. It is amazing to find an Augustine in such company. Much must be ascribed to circumstance. Thagaste and Carthage were out-of-the-way half-barbarous places. Augustine himself belonged to what we should call the lower middle class, was badly educated, and probably saw little of such exotic refinement as may have existed in the neighbourhood. But Manicheeism had undoubtedly a certain power. It gave a definite answer to just those doubts that were beginning to press upon Augustine's mind, a trenchant, uncompromising answer, such as young men love.

We need not draw the reader into the details of this singular system. They were purely absurd, consisting largely of wild Oriental fancies about matters that belong to the sober domain of physical science. For us they have no interest except that they finally helped Augustine out of his entanglement. Manicheeism gave its own account of the eclipses of the sun. Greek science gave another. Greek science was right because it could predict the eclipses. Therefore the science of Manicheeism was wrong. And, therefore again, Manicheeism was wrong universally. For its science was part of its theology, and its theology rested on exactly the same basis as its science. There is a grave lesson for us here. Those who condemned Galileo can hardly have been familiar with the *Confessions*.

Had these nightmare absurdities formed the whole of Mani's teaching, it would have been impossible to understand its curious vitality in the west. But it had also a moral side, and here lay the charm. It offered to Augustine the exact advice that at the moment he wanted

B

to receive. He asked whether he was really
called upon to believe the Hebrew Scriptures,
and the answer was, "You are not." Further,
this fiery, clever young man, disgusted with his
vices, yet not truly repentant, demanded how
far he was responsible for his evil deeds, whether
the sense of guilt was a reality or an illusion.
The answer was, "It is an illusion. You are
not responsible at all. You could not help
acting as you did, but come to us and we will
show you how to escape that degrading bondage."
Such an offer seemed well worth trying.

How Augustine escaped from the net he
explains with great clearness. He was dis-
appointed in the men. They had really nothing
to say for their own belief, and, when the great
Faustus, who was to resolve all difficulties,
appeared upon the scene, he proved to be as
ignorant, as vague, and as unsatisfactory as anybody else. Logic, science, common sense were
obviously not friendly to Manicheeism, but,
worst of all, those very tenets which had
attracted Augustine, and seemed as if they
must be true, broke down hopelessly when
he tried to make them work.

The Manichean system was nearly akin to
what we know in modern times as pessimism.
The world, it taught, is as bad as it can possibly
be. Nature, man's body and half of man's soul,
are the work of an evil God. Yet it also taught
that the good God is infinite. There was a
flagrant contradiction here which could not long
escape so keen a reasoner as Augustine. Nor,

from the moral point of view, could he rest satisfied with the assurance that evil is "a substance," some acrid humour in the blood, as it were, to be starved out by moral regimen, even if the moral regimen had been of a far more intelligent character than the ridiculous Manichee discipline. Nor again could he long believe that his own intelligence was, in fact, the Deity (iv. 15). The "pride" of the Manichees is obvious and colossal. They maintained in effect that they could have made the world infinitely better than it is.

The Manichees caught Augustine, we may say, upon the rebound. He began life with the easy optimism of youth. Nature, he had said to himself, is good—and of course he meant, as we all do, *my* nature. He had "followed nature," "worshipped nature," and she had plunged him into a boiling whirlpool. Now he burned his idol and declared nature—and again he meant *my* nature—to be evil. But against this the inner voice protested. If nature is evil, urged conscience, there is no guilt, and then why am I punished? Growing intelligence pointed in the same direction. If there be a God, it reasoned, He is Creator, and how can His own world be against Him? But most cogent of all was the protest of the heart. Shortly after his return from Carthage to Thagaste, Augustine lost a dearly loved friend (iv. 4). The anguish of bereavement forced upon him the question, What is love? and this again led him to ask, What is beauty? The moment he faced these thoughts he ceased to be a Manichee. For he could not examine them seriously without perceiving that there is beauty in everything, in all that his sect rejected, in the flesh, even in sin itself. Thus the moment Manicheeism was applied to the facts of experience it broke in his hand. It had no consolation to give. It could not even explain how sorrow begins, because it could not explain why we love anything or anybody. Far less could it read any meaning in sorrow itself. If grief purifies and elevates the spirit, if it takes men out of themselves and makes them one, as Christianity teaches, this was all a hopeless riddle to a theory which began and ended in dull and obstinate revolt. Thus again disappointment was Augustine's teacher. Manicheeism did not meet the facts, and here, more plainly perhaps than anywhere else, will be seen what is meant by the argument from Personality. The whole man rose against this futile dogmatism. Neither conscience, intellect, nor emotion could find sustenance in that barren land.

If nature is divine and law is the sign of God's presence, the conclusion is Platonism. If to these we add a third truth, that through sorrow lies the path of life, the conclusion is the Gospel. In other words, Platonism satisfies the intellect and the intellectual emotions, but the problems that gather round the will have never found any practical solution outside of the church. It is evident that Augustine was moving in the direction of one or the other. In fact, from the date of his arrival at Milan, he was occupied with both. But Platonism came first. It was, as he tells us, the vestibule through which he entered the church. Nor is this at all surprising. A theory of pain is a painful theory; most men postpone its acceptance as long as they can. Further, the history of Augustine's Manicheeism shews that he was as yet a tyro in philosophy; he needed more light on many important questions. And still further, he was as yet very ignorant as to what the church really taught. This seems surprising when we remember what a mother he had, but it is not so really. Monnica was a saint, but she was not an educated woman, and there were points on which she could neither guide, nor even understand, her gifted son. She could help only with prayers and tears. It was only later that Augustine came to understand that such a life is more valid than a syllogism.

The Platonism which Augustine studied seems to have been the *Enneads*, or some of the *Enneads*, of Plotinus, translated into Latin by that Victorinus Afer, of whose conversion so impressive a picture is given in the *Confessions*. From the greatest of Greek metaphysicians Augustine learned to see his way through a forest of difficulties that had hitherto blotted out the light. He learned from this heathen writer that "God is a Spirit," immaterial, eternal, unchangeable. Till now he had not been able to conceive of any substance that was not solid and extended. God had appeared to him as a vast luminous body, as a kind of subtle ether, diffused through all space. Henceforth he saw Him as the Soul

of souls and Life of lives.   Yet further the
Platonist taught him that this supreme Unity is
one, as the human spirit is one, or, even as the
human body is one, not with the logical unity of
absolute sameness, but with the real organic unity
of life, with a unity which admits of differences,
and of personal differences.   Three such personal
differences Plotinus admitted in the unity of the
Divine—the Good, the Intelligence and the
Soul.   The eternal Intelligence he called the
Creator.   All things exist by virtue of the divine
thought or "word," they are in so far as they
answer to the divine purpose.   How closely this
teaching corresponds to the opening of St John's
Gospel Augustine himself points out (vii. 9).
It is a great philosophy, perhaps the greatest that
human reason has ever attained to, and Augustine
seems to have thrown himself into it with aban-
donment.   He seems even to have become an
adept and attained to the Platonic Vision, for the
ecstasy in which "with the flash of one trembling
glance he arrived at THAT WHICH IS" (vii. 17)
is Plotinian and not Christian.

But, though Platonism satisfied the intelligence
and the æsthetic sense of Augustine, it could not
meet the demands of his conscience.   In Platonism things are nearer to God or further from
Him, more or less receptive of Him, but there
is no real distinction between good and evil.   It
amounts to the same thing, if we say that to the
Platonist the truly divine, the truly personal, is
the intellect alone.   God is the great Geometer,
eternally blessed in the contemplation of un-

clouded truth, but not the Father who loves or grieves over His children, not the Shepherd who calleth His own sheep by name. Such a Deity may satisfy those calm impersonal spirits who hardly know what evil is, and whose life has been happily sheltered from the storm, but Augustine's lot had been a fierce struggle with a deeply human problem. What he craved was not knowledge, but deliverance, Luther's *Deum quo confugiam*, and this he could find only in the Cross.

The Platonist held that moral evil can be got rid of by moral discipline. It did not affect the personality : it was like weeds and shells clinging to a statue that has lain for long at the bottom of the sea. Cleanse off this wrack and rubbish, and there is the statue as beautiful as ever. Augustine knew that this was not true, and here he parted company with Platonism. He knew that moral ignorance is not an accretion, but a taint. To the last he held with the Platonists that evil is "a privation," the absence of good which ought to be present, like blindness in a man. Hence, he speaks of evil as "nothing." But he looked upon this privation, this ignorance, this blindness as penal, as God's way of punishing rebellion. It was a mark of the divine displeasure, it was at once the cause and the effect of sin. And it could not be cured by mere moral gymnastics. All this he knew, not as a theorem, but as a matter of fact. He had probed the thing to the bottom, he had worked it out himself, and this was the ultimate result, not only *a* fact, but *the* fact.

He found the remedy in another fact, in the humiliation of Jesus Christ. How he found it he must relate for himself; there is here no need of any commentary. Only one point should be noticed. It has been asked sometimes whether he first found the light, or first renounced the world. St Augustine tells us expressly that the two aspects of his conversion were one in time and essence. As he read the words of St Paul, "as though his heart were flooded with a light of peace, all the shadows of doubt melted away (viii. 12)." Will and intellect shifted their centres at the same instant. At this supreme moment, as throughout the long process that led up to it, his personality was never divided. It never is divided except by way of abstraction.

There can be no doubt that Augustine, like Pascal, reached his conclusion by throwing his heart into the scales. Some count this a deadly sin against logic. The answer must be that the value of a logical conclusion depends upon the value of the premisses, and the value of the premisses depends upon the accuracy with which they represent all the facts. The object of this long introduction has been to explain the course of Augustine's reasoning, how he proceeded from one generalisation upon life to another, and found by experience that each was too narrow, until at last the question was fined down to the ultimate issue, "Am I to take account of the Christian facts or not?" Would he not have been illogical if he had refused to do so?

It will be seen that the difficulties besetting the theory of knowledge did not in any way affect St Augustine. He was perfectly well aware of their existence and their nature. Hume could have told him nothing new. He says quite frankly that religious belief is not capable of proof, or not to all men. Indeed, nothing that is of the slightest importance, no fact, is capable of proof. On what then did he repose? On Faith, no doubt, Faith built in the last resort on the evidence of his own personality. He saw law and order in the world, and he took it for granted that they flowed from a personality like his own. He found in revelation a theory of life which satisfied, not this or that requirement, but all the requirements of his complex nature, which explained not the grandeur only, nor the misery only, but both the grandeur and the misery of man. He found that this theory had great authority, that it was not merely taught by able men, but acted and carried out in practice, on an immense scale, by all kinds of people, with amazing thoroughness and confidence, and that it did, in fact, give to its votaries a peace and freedom, the secret of which was only partially apparent to those who studied it coolly from the outside. He took it for granted that this theory was true. Or shall we say that its truth was borne in upon him, that at a certain point a miraculous voice called to him in accents that could not be mistaken? And if so, how does this differ from that wonderful process by which any student, any practical man, who has long been poring over a set of refractory phenomena, suddenly grasps the law that explains them all? The simplest act of inference is quite inexplicable, and Augustine's conversion may have been miraculous without being in the least singular.

There are three leading ideas in the *Confessions* by which the reader may at once test the degree of his sympathy with the author. The first is expressed in the famous phrase, "Thou hast made us unto Thyself, and our heart is restless until it rests in Thee." This is the keynote of the whole book. The second is that truth is like food; if it is truth, it nourishes the whole nature of man. The third shall be given in Augustine's own words, "*Cibus sum grandium; cresce et manducabis Me.*" The food of the man is not the food of the child, the knowledge of the man is not the knowledge of the child. The student of life as a whole sees facts that escape the eye of the specialist; still more the expert understands things differently from the amateur, or even from the student. Practice without theory is of much value, but of what use is theory without practice in a ship upon the sea?

We live in an age of theories which come and go, ending in mere denials and divisions. Unity will cease to be no more than a golden dream in proportion as man comes to see in theory a thing to be worked out, to be applied thoroughly and consistently to the facts of life.

If you believe a thing, Materialism, Socialism, whatever it may be, go and do it; preach it and act it without scruple and without compromise.

Do not wait for others or serve the times. If your theory will not work, note carefully the point where it breaks down, cast it away at once, and try another. There is no truth for him who is not true to himself.

Perhaps this may be called the final lesson of the *Confessions*, and indeed of all Christian experience.

TABLE OF NECESSARY DATES.

A.D.

354. Augustine born at Thagaste on Nov. 13.

371. Death of his father, Patricius.

372. Birth of Augustine's son Adeodatus.

,, About this time he opened a school at Thagaste

376. He returned to Carthage and taught there.

383. He went to Rome and held classes there.

385. He was appointed public Rhetoric lecturer a Milan.

387. He was baptised at Milan with Alypius anc Adeodatus.

387. Death of his mother Monnica at Ostia.

388. Augustine returned to Africa.   Death of Adeodatus.

391. He was ordained priest at Hippo.

395. He was consecrated bishop of Hippo as coadjutor to Valerius.

396. Death of Valerius

397. Date of the *Confessions*.

430. Augustine died on Aug. 28, while the Vandals were besieging Hippo.

(The following passage is transcribed from the edition of William Watts).

St Augustine's owne testimony of this Booke taken out of his Retractations.

The thirteene bookes of my Confessions, both of my sinnes and good deedes, do prayse God, who is both just and good; and doe excite both the affection and vnderstanding of man towards him. In the meane time, forasmuch as concerneth me, they wrought this effect, when I wrote them, and so they yet do, when now I read them. What others find thereby, let themselves obscrue; but this I know, that they haue much pleased and do much please many of my brethren. From the first, thorow the whole tenth Booke they are written of myselfe; in the three Bookes following of the holy Scriptvre; from that place where it is sayd In the beginning God made heauen and earth, till he speaks of the Rest of the Sabbath. In the fourth booke, when I confessed the misery of my mind; upon occasion of my friend's death, saying That my soule was, as it were made one, of both our soules, and that therefore it was perhaps, that I feared to dye, lest he might wholy die, whom I extremely loued, this seemeth rather a light kinde of Declamation, then a Serious Confession. Though yet howsoeuer, that impertinency be somewhat moderated, by the addition of this word, perhaps, which then I used. And that also which I sayd in the thirteenth booke, The firmament was made, between those superiour spirituall waters, and these inferiour corporeall waters, was not consideratiuelly enough expressed. But the truth heerof, is extremely hard to be discouered. This worke beginneth thus: Great art thou, O Lord, and highly worthy to be praysed.

BOOK I

CALLING upon the Name of the Lord,
Augustine records the beginnings
of his life. He acknowledges
the sins of infancy and of boyhood; and confesses that at this
time he was fonder of games and
childish delights than of study.

CHAPTER I

He will praise God, being prompted thereto by God; and considers whether prayer comes before praise, or praise before prayer.

GREAT art Thou, O Lord, and highly to be praised;[1] great is Thy power, yea, and Thy wisdom is infinite.[2] And man would praise Thee, because he is one of Thy creatures; yea, man—though he bears about with him his mortality, the proof of his sin, the proof that Thou, O God, dost resist the proud[3]—yet would man praise Thee, because he is one of Thy creatures. Thou dost prompt us thereto, making it a joy to praise Thee; for Thou hast created us unto Thyself, and our heart finds no rest until it rests in Thee. Grant me, Lord, to know and understand which comes first, to call upon Thee, or to praise Thee, and which comes first, to know Thee or to call upon Thee.

2. But who can call upon Thee, that knows Thee not? For they who know Thee not may call upon Thee by names that are not Thine. Or must we call upon Thee that Thou mayst be known. Yet how shall they call upon Him in whom they have not believed, or how shall

[1] Ps. cxlv. 3.   [2] Ps. cxlvii. 5.   [3] 1 Pet. v. 5.

C

they believe without a preacher?[1] And they shall praise the Lord that seek Him.[2] For they that seek will find Him,[3] and they that find will praise Him. Let me seek Thee, O Lord, by calling, let me call through believing on Thee; for unto us hast Thou been preached. It is my faith that calls upon Thee, O Lord, my faith, which Thou gavest, which Thou didst infuse, by the Humanity of Thy Son, by the ministry of Thy Preacher.

CHAPTER II

He recognizes that God to whom he prays is in him, and that he is in God.

AND how shall I call upon my God, my God and Lord. For in truth when I call upon Him I call Him to enter into me. And what place is there in me into which my God can come; into which God, the God who made heaven and earth, can come and dwell in me? Is there, indeed, O Lord my God, is there aught in me that can contain Thee? Nay, even the heaven and the earth—which Thou hast created and wherein Thou hast created me—can they contain Thee?

2. Or does everything that is contain Thee? for without Thee nothing that is could be. Why then do I pray that thou shouldest enter into

[1] Rom. x. 14.   [2] Ps. xxii. 26.   [3] Matt. vii. 7.

me seeing that I also am. For I should not be, if Thou wert not in me. For I am not in hell, yet Thou art even there. For, though I go down into hell, Thou art there also.[1] I should not be then, O my God, I should not be at all, unless Thou wert in me. Or rather I should not be, if I were not in Thee of whom are all things, through whom are all things, in whom are all things.[2] Even so, Lord, even so. Whither then do I call Thee, seeing that I am in Thee? Or whence canst Thou come into me? For whither can I fly beyond heaven and earth, that my God, who hath said, I fill heaven and earth,[3] should thence come into me.

CHAPTER III

God is wholly everywhere, yet so that nothing contains the whole of God.

DO heaven and earth then contain Thee, since Thou fillest them? Or dost Thou fill them and overflow, since they do not contain Thee? And whither dost Thou overflow, when heaven and earth are filled? Or dost Thou not need any limit to contain Thee, since Thou containest all; for what thou fillest, Thou fillest by containing? For the vessels which are full of Thee do not confine Thee; though they should be shattered, Thou wouldest not be

[1] Ps. cxxxix. 7. [2] Rom. xi. 36. [3] Jer. xxiii. 24.

ured out. And when Thou art poured out
pon us,[1] Thou art not debased but we are
exalted, Thou gatherest us yet art not scat-
tered. But when Thou fillest all things, dost
Thou fill them with all Thyself?

2. Or because all things cannot contain the
whole of Thee, do they receive a part of Thee,
and do all receive the same part at the same
time? Or does each receive its own part,
greater things a greater part, lesser things a
lesser? Then is one part of Thee greater,
another less. Or art Thou wholly everywhere,
though naught receives the whole of Thee?

CHAPTER IV

The Majesty, and ineffable Perfection of God.

WHAT art Thou then, my God, what, I
ask, save the Lord God. For what
God is there but the Lord, or what God but our
God.[2] Highest, best, most mighty, most almighty; most merciful, most just; most far,
and yet most near; fairest, yet strongest; fixed,
yet incomprehensible: unchangeable, yet changing
all things; never new, yet never aged; renewing
all, yet bringing the haughty into decrepitude and
they know it not. Ever busy, yet ever at rest;

[1] Joel ii. 28.
[2] Ps. xviii. 31 agreeing with Ps. xvii. 32 of the
Vulgate.

gathering, yet never needing; bearing, filling, guarding: creating, nourishing, perfecting; seeking, though Thou hast no lack.

2. Love is Thine without passion, jealousy without alarms, repentance without sorrow, anger without disorder. Thou changest Thy works, but not Thy purpose; Thou takest what Thou findest, and dost never lose. Never poor art Thou, yet delighting in gain: never covetous, yet exacting usury. Men give Thee more than Thou dost claim, that Thou shouldest be their debtor, yet who possesses aught that is not Thine? Thou payest debts which Thou dost not owe; Thou forgivest debts and losest nothing. What can I say, my God, my life, my holy joy? Or what can any one say, when he speaks of Thee? And woe to them that praise Thee not, since they who praise Thee most are no better than dumb.

CHAPTER V

He prays for the love of God, and pardon for his sins.

WHO can grant me this boon that I should be at peace in Thee, that Thou shouldest enter into my heart and intoxicate it, that I should forget my evils and clasp Thee, my one and only good? What art Thou unto me? Have pity upon me that I may tell. What am I unto Thee that Thou shouldest bid me love hee, that Thou shouldest be wroth and menace me with unutterable woe if I love Thee not? Not to love Thee—is not that in itself a great woe? O, by Thy loving kindness, tell me, O Lord my God, what Thou art unto me. Say unto my soul I am thy salvation,[1] say it so that I may hear. Behold the ears of my soul are before Thee, O Lord; open them, and say unto my soul I am thy salvation. I will run after this voice and lay hold of Thee. Hide not Thy face from me. Let me die lest I die, that I may see Thy face.

2. The house of my soul is narrow; O enlarge it that Thou mayest enter in. It is ruinous, O repair it. It displeases Thy sight; I confess it, I know. But who shall cleanse it, or unto whom shall I cry but unto Thee? Cleanse me from my secret faults, O Lord, and spare Thy servant from strange sins.[2] I believe, and therefore do I speak.[3] O Lord, Thou knowest. Have I not confessed unto Thee mine own sins to my own confusion, O my God, and Thou hast forgiven the impiety of my heart.[4] I strive not in judgment with Thee [5] who art truth: and I will not deceive myself, lest my iniquity should lie unto itself.[6] I will not contend with Thee

[1] Ps. xxxv. 3.

[2] Ps. xix. 12-13 agreeing with Ps. xviii. 13-14 of the Latin Vulgate.

[3] Ps. cxvi. 10.

[4] Ps. xxxii. 5, but differing from both English and Vulgate.

[5] Job ix. 2.

[6] Ps. xxvii. 12 agreeing with xxvi. 12 of the Vulgate.

in judgment, for if Thou, O Lord, art extreme
to mark what is done amiss, O Lord, who may
abide? [1]

CHAPTER VI

*He describes his infancy, praising the providence
and eternity of God.*

YET suffer me to speak before Thy mercy, me
who am but dust and ashes. Yea, suffer
me to speak, for, behold, I speak not to man who
scorns me, but to Thy mercy. Even Thou perhaps dost scorn me, but Thou wilt turn and have
pity. [2] For what is it that I would say, O Lord
my God, save that I know not whence I came
hither into this dying life, shall I call it, or living
death? And the comforts of Thy pity received
me, as I have heard from the father and mother
of my flesh, from whom and in whom Thou
didst fashion me in time: for I do not recollect.
And so the comfort of human milk was ready
for me. For my mother and my nurses did not
fill their own bosoms, but Thou, O Lord, by
their instrumentality gavest me the food of infancy, according to Thy ordinance, out of the
riches which Thou hast shed abroad to the
farthest rim of creation. Thy gift it was that I
asked no more than Thou gavest; that my
nurses gladly gave to me what Thou gavest them.

[1] Ps. cxxx 3. [2] Jer. xii. 15.

For Thou didst ordain the affection whereby they gladly gave to me that wherein Thou madest them to abound. For this was good for them, and my food flowed from them, yet not from them, but through them. For, of a truth, all goods come from Thee, O God; and from my God is all my health.[1] This I learned afterwards, when Thou didst loudly call to me by all Thy benefits, within me and without. For in those days I could but suck and feel pleasure, and weep at fleshly pain; nothing more. Afterwards I began also to smile, at first in sleep, then awake. For this I have been told and believe, since I see other babies do the same. But I do not recollect how it was with myself.

2. And behold gradually I came to know where I was, and I tried to express my wants to those who could gratify them, yet could not, because my wants were inside me, and they were outside, nor had they any power of getting into my soul. And so I made movements and sounds, signs like my wants, the few I could, the best I could; for they were not really like my meaning. And when I was not obeyed, because people did not understand me, or because they would not do me harm, I was angry because elders did not submit to me, because freemen would not slave for me, and I avenged myself on them by tears. The babies that I have seen are like this, and such was I also. Babies who knew not, have taught me what I have been, better than my own nurses who knew. And, lo, my infancy has

[1] 2 Sam. xxiii. 5 not verbally.

long been dead, and I live. But Thou, O Lord, who ever livest and in whom nothing ever dies—for before the first beginning of time, before all that can even be called "before," Thou art, and art God and Lord of all that Thou hast created, and in Thy sight stand fast the causes of the transient, and the fountains of the changeable abide unchanged, and the reasons of the unreasoning and temporal live eternally—tell me, I beseech Thee, O God, and have mercy on my misery, for I am Thine, tell me whether another life of mine died before my infancy began, or only that which I spent in the womb of my mother? For about that something has been told me, and I have seen women with child.

3. Even before this what was there, O my joy, my God? Was I anywhere, was I anyone? Nowhere can I find the answer, not from father or mother, not from the experience of others, not from my own memory. Dost Thou mock me, when I ask this of Thee, bidding me praise Thee, and confess myself unto Thee, for what I know. I will confess unto Thee, O Lord of heaven and earth, and I will praise Thee for my birth and infancy, which I cannot remember. Thou dost enable man to gather from the lot of others how it was in his own case, and to believe much about himself from the testimony even of weak women. For I was, and was alive even then, and, before infancy had reached its close, I was seeking for signs to make known my feelings to others. Whence came so wondrous a creature but from Thee, O Lord?

Can anyone make himself? Can the stream of being and of life, that runs into us, derive from any other fountain? No, Thou dost make us, O Lord, whose being and whose life are ever the same, because Thou art nothing else than [1] supreme being, supreme life. For Thou art the highest and changest not,[2] nor does To-day run out its hours in Thee; and yet in Thee its hours run out, for in Thee is every moment of time. For they would have no path to fly by, if Thou didst not contain them all. And since Thy years shall not fail,[3] Thy years are one To-day. How many days of mine and of my fathers have passed through Thy To-day, from Thy eternity received their mode of being, and existed after their fashion! And others again will pass, and receive their mode of being, and exist after their fashion. But Thou art the same[4]; the work of to-morrow and the days after, the work of yesterday and the days before, Thou wilt do To-day, Thou hast done To-day. What care I if any miss my meaning? Let him too rejoice, while he says What thing is this?[5] Let him rejoice even so, and desire rather by missing to find, than by finding to miss Thee.

[1] *idipsum*, a verbal reference to Ps. iv. 9 (Latin). See note on p. 307 below.
[2] Mal. iii. 6.
[3] Ps. cii. 27.
[4] Ps. cii. 27.
[5] Ex. xvi. 15, agreeing with the Vulgate (*Manhu? quod significat : Quid est hoc?*).

CHAPTER VII

Even infancy is not without sin.

HEAR me, O God. Woe to the sins of
men! And man can speak like this, and
Thou dost pity him, for Thou didst make him,
yet didst not make his sin. Who can tell me
the sin of my infancy? For none is clean from
sin in Thy sight, not even the infant whose life
upon earth is but one day long. Who can tell
me? Shall I not reply, Any tiny little creature
in whom I see what I cannot recollect? How
then did I sin? Was it that I craved with tears
for the breast? For if I were now to crave so
greedily, not for the breast but for dainties suited
to my years, most justly should I be ridiculed
and blamed. Even then, therefore, I deserved
blame; but custom and reason saved me from
blame, because I could not understand it. For
we root out and cast away these childish ways
as we grow. Yet I never saw anyone who tried
to mend by casting away what he knew to be
good. Or may we say that for the time it was
good to beg with tears what could only hurt if
given, to fly into a passion because freemen,
elders, parents would not humour a whim,
because the wise would not run at our beck
and call, to try to strike and hurt with all
our might because our sovereign will was not
obeyed, though it could not be obeyed except

to our harm? If so, the innocence of infancy depends on the weakness of its limbs, not on its character. I know, because I have seen, jealousy in a babe. It could not speak, yet it eyed its twin brother with pale cheeks and look of hate.

2. This is common knowledge. Mothers and nurses say that they make atonement for these faults—by what remedies they know best. Can we say that this, too, is innocence, in that plentiful and abounding fount of milk to suffer no rival, though he, too, is in dire need, and depends for his life on that one sustenance? But these faults, though they are faults, and grave faults, are borne with a smile, because they will drop off with time. Still though this may seem right, consider that these very same things could not be tolerated in after years. Thou, therefore, O Lord my God, who givest to the infant life, and the body we see, equipped with senses, compacted with members, adorned with shape, furnished with all the capacities of sentient existence for its completeness and its safety—Thou dost bid me praise Thee in this, and confess unto Thee and sing unto Thy Name, O Thou most Highest.[1] For Thou art God, Almighty and Good, even though Thou hadst made nothing else but these things of earth, which none could have made but Thou alone, from whom comes every mode of being, Thou Fairest, who makest all things fair, whose law is the rule of all the world.

[1] Ps. xcii. 1.

3. My infancy then, O Lord, which I do not
remember, which I know by hearsay, which I am
aware that I lived from observation of other
infants (a sure and certain ground of inference)
—my infancy I say, I am loth to count as a
part of the life which I live in this world. For
it lies as deep in the darkness of oblivion as that
which I passed in my mother's womb. But, if
I was conceived in iniquity, and in sin did my
mother nourish me in her womb,[1] where I
beseech Thee, O my God, where, O Lord,
where or when was I Thy servant innocent ?
But, lo, I pass over that time. I can no longer
track its course, and what have I now to do
with it ?

CHAPTER VIII

How, as a boy, he learned to talk.

DID I not, on my journey hence from infancy,
come to boyhood, or rather did not boyhood come to me, and take the place of infancy ?
Infancy did not depart (for whither could it go ?)
and yet it ceased to be. I was no longer a
speechless infant, but a speaking boy. This I
remember, and afterwards I observed how I
learned to talk. I was not taught by elders
supplying me with words in a regular course of

[1] Ps. li. 7, but differing from both English and
Vulgate.

instruction, as later on I acquired literature, but I myself, by means of the intelligence which Thou gavest me, O my God, endeavouring by cries and all kinds of noises and gestures to make known my feelings and get my desires, finding that my meaning could not be conveyed by signs, or that my signs could not convey it, began to grasp in my memory the names by which those about me called a thing. When they pronounced the word and then touched the object, I watched, and I understood that the sound which they made, when they desired to point out a thing, was the name which they gave to that thing.

2. That such was their intention was evident to me from their movements, that primitive language common to all mankind, which talks by looks, and acting, and sounds expressive of liking or disliking, wanting or shunning. Thus gradually I acquired a store of words arranged in sentences, and by frequent repetition I came to perceive of what things they were symbols, and, by training my mouth to their utterance, I gained the power of verbal expression. So I exchanged with those about me the signals of meaning, and launched out upon the stormy sea of human fellowship, while still depending on the authority of parents and the direction of elders.

CHAPTER IX

*The hatred of learning, the love of play, and fear
of flogging in boys.*

O GOD, my God, what misery did I then
endure, what deception! For it was
held up to me, as the whole duty of a boy, to
obey those who exhorted me to get on in this
world, and make a name in wordy arts, which
minister to the glory of man and deceitful riches.
Then was I sent to school to learn letters.
Alas, I knew not what profit they were, and
yet I was flogged, if I was slow to learn. For
this was the good old way. Those who have
lived this life before us laid out thorny paths
which we were compelled to tread, so sorely are
labour and pain multiplied for the sons of
Adam.

2. Yet we met with men who prayed to Thee,
O Lord, and from them we learned to feel (as
well as boys could feel), that Thou art some
great One, that Thou couldst hear us and help,
though we could not see Thee. For, even as a
boy, I began to pray to Thee, my Help and my
Refuge; to call upon Thee I burst the bonds of
my tongue, and prayed to Thee—child as I was,
how passionately!—that I might not be flogged
at school. Thou didst not hear me, yet
countedst it not for folly unto me;[1] but my

[1] Ps. xxii. 2, agreeing with xxi. 3 of the Vulgate.

elders, and even my parents, who wished me
nothing but good, laughed at my stripes, my
great and grievous ill.   Is there anyone, O
Lord, so high in spirit, so bound to Thee by
lofty devotion—is there anyone at all, for even
want of feeling may give courage—is there a
man who by filial adhesion to Thee is made so
stout of heart, that he despises racks and hooks
and the whole arsenal of torture, which all men
shrink from with horror and prayers for deliverance, and laughs at the cruel executioner, as
our own parents laughed at the torments inflicted
on their children by the schoolmaster?   Certainly we feared them as much, and prayed
as earnestly that we might escape them.   And
yet we were sinning, when we wrote less, or
read less, or thought less about our lessons than
was expected of us.

   3. For I had no want, O Lord, of memory
or capacity—these Thou gavest me in full measure
for that age—but we loved play, and for this we
were punished, by those who surely were doing
the same thing.   But the follies of elders are
called business, while the business of children is
punished by grown men ; and no one pities boy
or man or both.   Can any reasonable person
think it right that a boy should be flogged for
playing at ball, because play hinders him in the
acquisition of knowledge, with which he is only
to play a baser game in after years?   Or was
there anything to choose between me and the
master who flogged me?   For he, if his fellow-
teacher worsted him in some pedantic dispute,

N.B

was more disordered by rage and envy, than
I, when beaten by my playmate in a game of
catch.

CHAPTER X

*By love of play and shows he is tempted away
from the pursuit of learning.*

AND yet I was sinning, O Lord God, Thou
Ruler and Creator of all nature, but Ruler
only of sin. O Lord my God, I was sinning,
in that I resisted the commands of my parents
and my teachers. For I might employ for a
good purpose that education which my guardians
may have wished me to acquire for a base one.
Nor was it the deliberate choice of a better way
that made me refractory, but the love of amusement and the pride of winning. Again there
was the wish to tickle my ears with fiction, that
they might itch the more, and the same spirit of
curiosity danced in my eyes, as they gazed upon
the shows and games of elder people. Strange,
that those who exhibit games should be invested
with a dignity which almost all parents covet for
their sons, and yet that a father should suffer his
son to be beaten, if the games have tempted the
boy to neglect the learning, which is to enable
him to exhibit shows in his turn! Look
upon this, O Lord, in Thy mercy, and deliver
us who call upon Thee. Deliver those also

D

who call upon Thee not, that they may call upon Thee, and that Thou mayest deliver them.

CHAPTER XI

In his sickness he prays for Baptism, which his mother purposely defers.

FOR I had heard, while yet a boy, of the eternal life promised to us through the humility of Thy Son, our Lord God, who condescended to our pride. Even from the womb of my mother, whose sure hope was in Thee, I was signed with the sign of His Cross, and seasoned with His salt. Thou sawest, O Lord, when one day, while I was yet a boy, a fit of indigestion threw me into a sudden fever, and I was like to die—Thou sawest, O my God, for Thou wast already my Guardian, with what eagerness and faith I implored, from the love of my mother and of Thy Church, the mother of us all, the baptism of Thy Christ, my God and Lord. She, the mother of my flesh, whose chaste and faithful heart travailed so anxiously for the birth of my eternal salvation, was filled with alarm, and was arranging in haste that I should be initiated and washed by Thy wholesome sacraments, confessing Thee, O Lord Jesus, for the remission of sins, when suddenly I revived. And so my cleansing was deferred, as it seemed certain that I should be still further defiled, since I was to live; because, forsooth, after that bath the guilt and the vileness of sin would be greater and more perilous.

2. Thus I was already a believer, and so was my mother, and the whole family, except my father; yet did he not prevail over the power of a mother's love, nor was my faith the weaker, because he did not at that time believe. For it was her set purpose that Thou shouldest be a father unto me, O my God, and in this, by Thy help, she overcame her husband, whom she obeyed though she was his superior, because in this she was obeying Thy clear command. Gladly would I know, O my God—if it were Thy pleasure to instruct me—why my baptism was then deferred. Was the rein laid loose upon my neck for my own good? or was it not laid loose? If not, how is it that we so constantly hear people say, "Let him do what he likes; he is not yet baptised." Yet, where the body's health is concerned, we do not say "Let him be wounded again; he is not yet healed." Far better if I had been quickly healed, if both I and my parents had taken heed that the health of my soul should be restored and safe in the keeping of Thee, its Giver. Yes, far better. But my mother already foresaw the billows of temptation, that were to break over me as soon as my boyhood was past. And so she preferred to risk on them the clay of which I was to be shaped, rather than the Image of God itself.

CHAPTER XII

How he was driven to learn from wrong motives,
which yet God turned to good.

YET in my boyhood (which my parents
thought a less dangerous age than that of
adolescence) I did not love learning, and I hated
being driven towards it; yet I was driven, and it
was well for me, though I was not doing well:
for I would not learn except perforce. Now no
one does well against his will, even if what he
does is well. Nor were those who drove me
doing well, yet was I well dealt with by Thee,
O my God. For they could discern no other
use for the learning, which they forced upon me,
than the gratification of the insatiable craving for
gilded poverty and shameful glory.

2. But Thou, who numberest every hair of
our heads,[1] didst turn to my profit the error of
those who forced me to learn; and my own
error, my reluctance to learn, Thou turnedst to
my chastisement, for well did I deserve to suffer,
who was so small a child, and yet so great a
sinner. And so by the hands of those who did
me ill, Thou wast doing me well, and by my own
sin thou wast justly requiting me. For Thou
hast commanded that an ill regulated mind should
be its own punishment; and it is so.

[1] Matt. x. 30.

CHAPTER XIII

In what studies he found most delight.

BUT even now I cannot understand why I
hated Greek, which I was taught in my
earliest school-days. Because I loved Latin—the
literature, I mean, not the grammar. For the
first lessons of the Latin schools, in which one
learns to read, write and multiply, I thought as
dull and penal as Greek from first to last. Now
why was this, if not from sin and vanity of life,
because I was flesh and a spirit that goeth and
returneth not? [1] For certainly the first lessons,
which formed in me the enduring power of reading books and writing what I choose, were better,
because more solid, than the later, in which I was
obliged to learn by heart the wanderings of
Æneas, forgetting my own wanderings, and to
weep for the death of Dido, who slew herself
for love, while I looked with dry eyes on my
own most unhappy death, wandering far from
Thee, O God, my Life. For what is so pitiful
as an unhappy wretch who pities not himself,
who has tears for the death of Dido, because
she loved Æneas, but none for his own death,
because he loves not Thee!

3. O God, the light of my heart, Thou

[1] Ps. lxxviii. 39, but differing from both English
and Vulgate.

hidden bread of my soul, Thou mighty Husband of my mind and of the bosom of my thought, I loved Thee not. I lived in adultery away from Thee, and all men cried unto me, Well done! well done! For the friendship of this world is adultery against Thee.[1] Well done! well done! men cry, till one is ashamed not to be even as they. For this I had no tears, but I could weep for Dido, "slain with the sword and flying to the depths,"[2] while I was myself flying from Thee into the depths of Thy creation, earth returning to earth. And, if I was forbidden to read these tales, I grieved; because I might not read what caused me grief. Such lessons were thought more elevating and profitable than mere reading or writing. What madness is this!

3. But now let Thy truth, O my God, cry aloud in my soul, and say unto me Not so, not so; the earlier teaching was the better. For, lo, I would far rather forget the wanderings of Aeneas, and everything of the kind, than how to read and write. Truly over the door of the grammar-school there hangs a curtain, yet is that curtain the shroud of falsehood not the veil of mysteries. Let not those, whom no longer I fear, cry out against me, while I confess unto Thee, O my God, the promptings of my soul, and acquiesce in the condemnation of my evil ways, that I may love Thy good ways. Let not the buyers or sellers of grammar cry out against me. Because if I

[1] An allusion to James iv. 4.
[2] *Virg. Aen.* vi. 457.

were to ask them whether the poet speaks the
truth, when he says that Aeneas came to Carthage,
the unlearned would answer that they do not
know, the learned that he does not.

4. But, if I were to ask how the name of
Aeneas is spelled, all who have learned spelling
would answer rightly, in accordance with the
convention by which men have regulated the use
of the alphabet. And again, if I were to ask
which it would be most inconvenient to forget,
the art of reading and writing or these poetic
fictions, who does not see what answer a man
would be obliged to give, unless he had wholly
forgotten himself? I was sinning then when,
as a boy, I preferred those vanities to more
useful arts, or rather when I loved the one
and hated the other. "One and one two,
two and two four" I thought a wearisome
drone, but the wooden horse teeming with
armed men, the flames of Troy, the ghost
of Creusa—these were the vain delights that
enchanted me.

CHAPTER XIV

How he hated Greek.

WHY then did I hate my Greek literature,
which was full of such songs. For
Homer also weaves these fables with a skilful
hand, nor is any vanity so delightful as his. Yet

he was distasteful to me as a boy, and so I think would Virgil be to Greek boys, if they were compelled to learn him in the same way, that is to say, by dint of drudgery. The drudgery of acquiring a foreign tongue turned all the sweetness of the Grecian myths into gall. For I knew none of the words, and I was forced to master them by menaces and punishment. There was a time when I knew no Latin words, when I was an infant; but I learned them by merely attending, without fear or pain, amid caresses, laughter and joy, from nurses, friends and playmates.

2. I learned them, I say, without the dread of punishment to spur me on, because my own heart was eager to bring its ideas to light, and could not do so till I had acquired some little store of phrases, not from teachers but from talkers, in whose ears I in turn was travailing to express my thoughts. It is plain then that the freedom of curiosity is a far better instructor in language than the compulsion of fear. Yet fear restrains the vagaries of curiosity by Thy laws, O God, Thy laws which begin with the schoolmaster's rod, and end with the martyr's fiery trial, Thy laws which have power to mingle a wholesome bitterness in our cup, calling us back to Thee, away from the fatal delights that tempted us to leave Thee.

CHAPTER XV

A Prayer for the Love of God.

HEAR, O Lord, my petition and suffer not
my soul to faint beneath Thy chastisement.
Suffer me not to faint in confessing to Thee the
loving-kindness, whereby Thou didst rescue me
from all my evil ways. Be Thou sweeter to me
than all the allurements which I once pursued:
that I may love Thee with all my strength, and
clasp Thy hand with all my heart, so that I may
be delivered from all temptation even unto the end.

2. For behold, O Lord, my King and my
God, to Thy service I devote whatever useful
thing I learned as a boy, my speaking, my
writing, my reading, my arithmetic. For, when
I learned vain things, Thou wast disciplining me,
and the sin of my delight in those vanities Thou
hast forgiven. For even in them I learned many
useful words, words that can be used with effect
in matters that are not vain ; and that is the safe
path for boys to walk in.

CHAPTER XVI

*He disapproves of the way in which boys are
taught.*

BUT woe to thee thou torrent of Use and
Wont ! Who can resist thee ? How long
vilt thou not be dried up, how long wilt thou

sweep away the sons of Eve into that vast and
stormy sea, which scarcely those who have
embarked upon the Tree[1] can cross in safety?
Was it not in thy book that I read of Jove, the
thunderer and the adulterer? Yet how could
he be both? These tales were told only that
the forged thunder might help and exculpate real
adulterers. Which of our longrobed professors
would listen patiently to a man, made out of the
same dust as themselves, who should cry "These
are fictions; Homer made God like man!
Would he had rather made man like God."[2]
But to speak the whole truth, these fictions,
for such they are, ascribe divinity to de-
bauched men, in order that debauchery might
no longer be counted debauchery, and that
the libertine might seem to emulate, not the
worst of men but the very Gods in heaven.

2. Yet, thou hellish torrent, the sons of men
are tossed about in thee, and pay high fees to
learn these lessons. And is it not a great
disaster, when such instruction is given publicly
in the market-place, in sight of the laws which
promise the apt scholar a salary much higher
than his fees? Thou roarest against thy rocks
crying, "I teach words; I give eloquence, the
power of persuasive expression." But is it so?
Should we not understand these words, "shower

---

[1] *Lignum* might be used either of the Ark or of the
Cross. There is an allusion here to Wisdom xiv. 5,
*propter hoc etiam et exiguo ligno credunt homines animas suas,
et transeuntes mare per ratem liberati sunt.*

[2] Cic. *Tusc.*, i. 26.

of gold," "lap," "trick," "temples of heaven,"
unless Terence brought upon the stage a pro-
fligate youth, justifying his uncleanness by the
example of Jove, as he gloats over a picture
painted on the wall, a picture to illustrate the
tale how "Jove rained into the lap of Danae a
shower of gold, and so the girl was tricked?"
See how he emboldens his lust by use of a
divine authority!

3. "Aye, and what a God," he goes on,
"He who shakes the temples of heaven with the
crashing thunder. Was not I, poor man, to
follow suit? That I did, right merrily." [1]
Certainly you need not sin in the same way to
learn those words more easily, but by the words
you learn to sin more boldly. I blame, not the
words, which are, indeed, elect and precious
vessels of thought, but the wine of error, which
in them was held to our lips by drunken teachers.
If we did not drink, we were beaten; nor
could we appeal to any sober judge. And
yet, O my God, in whose sight all my
reminiscences are now free from dread, I
conned these fables willingly, and, alas, with
delight, and for this I was pronounced a
hopeful scholar.

[1] Terence. *Eun.* iii. 5. 36-43.

CHAPTER XVII

Further strictures on the way in which boys are taught literature.

SUFFER me also, O my God, to tell in what absurdities I frittered away my talent, which was Thy gift. One task was set me that sorely troubled my mind, that under promise of praise or of censure, and even of stripes, I should declaim the speech of Juno, wrathful and sad, because she could not drive away from Italy the Teucrian King. I had been told that Juno had never uttered the words, but we were all compelled to trace the wandering footprints of the poet's fancy, and say in bald prose what he had sung in verse. And he spoke his piece with most applause, who best acted the passions of wrath and sorrow, with due respect to the dignity of the character, and clothed the sentiments in appropriate words.

2. Now why did it befal me, O my true life, my God, that my recitation was applauded above those of my equals and classmates? Are not such triumphs but vapour and wind? Was there no other field in which my talent and my tongue might have found occupation? Thy praises, O Lord, Thy praises, displayed in Thy Holy Scriptures, should have propped the climbing vine of my heart; it should not have blown loose amid idle trifles, a sport for the fowls of the air. For there is more than one way of sacrificing to the fallen angels.

CHAPTER XVIII

Men obey the laws of grammar, and disobey the laws of God.

BUT what wonder, if I plunged into vanities and abandoned Thy house, O my God, when I was taught to emulate men, who blushed for a barbarism or a solecism in the expression of some harmless fact, but plumed themselves on the purity and perspicacity, the fluency and brilliance of the speech, in which they revealed their own pollution. Thou seest these things, O Lord, long-suffering and plenteous in mercy and in truth,[1] Thou seest and keepest silence. Wilt Thou keep silence for ever? Even now Thou dost pluck out of this bottomless pit the soul that seeketh Thee, and thirsteth for Thy pleasures, and saith unto Thee, " I have sought Thy face ; Thy face, Lord, will I seek."[2] For I had gone far from Thy face in the darkness of my heart.

2. For not by the movement of our feet, and not by spaces that can be measured, do we fly from Thee or return to Thee? Did that younger son of Thine hire horse or chariot or ship,[3] did he fly on real wings, or walk with real legs to that far-off land where he spent in riotous

---

[1] Ps. lxxxvi. 15.
[2] Ps. xxvii. 8, but differing from both English and Vulgate.
[3] A reminiscence of Plotinus *Ennead,* i. 5, 8.

N.B.

R.

living all that Thou gavest at his setting forth? In love Thou gavest, O Father; in greater love Thou forgavest the returning prodigal. A lustful heart is that far-off land, a land of darkness, far from Thy face. Behold, O Lord, behold patiently, as is Thy wont, how scrupulously men observe the covenant of letters and syllables received from the speakers of old, how carelessly they disobey the eternal covenant of everlasting life received from Thee. One who believes and teaches the time-honoured laws of pronunciation, if against the rule of grammar he says 'uman for human, gives more offence to his fellow-creatures than if, in violation of Thy laws, he hated the human race, to which he himself belongs. As if, forsooth, an enemy were more deadly than the hatred which regards him as an enemy, or as if a man by his malice could destroy another more utterly than he destroys his own soul.

3. Assuredly the laws of language are not written so deeply on our hearts as the rule of conscience: "Do not to another what thou wouldst not that he should do unto thee." How dost Thou hide Thyself, O God, Thou only great, that dwellest in high places [1] in silence, and by an unfailing ordinance sendest penal blindness on lawless passion. A man seeking the glory of eloquence, in presence of a man who is judge, surrounded by bystanders who are men, while he inveighs against his adversary with the bitterest hatred, will be most carefully on his guard lest by a slip of the tongue he should say "men

[1] Isaiah xxxiii. 5.

was," [1] but will take no care at all lest, through the madness of his own soul, a man should perish from among men.

CHAPTER XIX

How the vices of boyhood pass over into later life.

SUCH was the threshold of my moral life, such my training for this scene of strife. I was more afraid of uttering a barbarism than of envying those who did not. All these faults I confess unto Thee, O my God, but they were thought merits by those whose approbation was my standard of excellence. For I could not see the gulf of vileness in which I was cast away from Thine eyes. [2] For in those eyes who was viler than I? nay, even the vile condemned me, for I practised innumerable deceits on my pedagogue, my masters, my parents, from love of play, from a passion for idle diversions, from a restless desire to imitate the follies of the theatre.

2. I even stole more than once from my father's cellar, and from the table, at the bidding of my greediness, or that I might have something to give to other boys, who sold me their play, though they loved it as much as I. And in my play I often sought to get the mastery by

[1] *inter hominibus* is the particular blunder which Augustine uses as an instance.

[2] Ps. xxxi. 22.

cheating, when I was myself mastered by the
vain desire to excel. Yet what did I so detest
as the very tricks which I played upon others,
and what did I so angrily denounce, when I
found them out? But, if I was myself found
out, I would fly into a passion rather than give
way.

3. Is this the innocence of boyhood? It is
not, O Lord, it is not. I cry to Thee for
pardon, O my God. As we disobeyed peda-
gogues and masters for nuts and balls and
sparrows, so in riper years we disobey governors
and kings for gold, for manors, for slaves; and
so heavier penalties take the place of the cane.
It was then humility, symbolised by the littleness
of childhood, which Thou wast commending,
when Thou saidst, "Of such is the Kingdom of
Heaven."[1]

CHAPTER XX

He gives thanks to God for the blessings of boyhood.

AND yet, O Lord my God, Thou best and
most excellent Creator and Ruler of the
world, I should owe Thee thanks, even though
Thou hadst wished that I should never be more
than boy. For I was; I was alive; I could
feel; I could guard my personality, the imprint[2]

---

[1] Matt. xix. 14.
[2] *Vestigium*, The phrase comes from Plotinus.

of that mysterious unity from which my being was derived; by my inner sense I could warrant the accuracy of my outer senses; I found delight in truth, even in little things and in reflections upon little things; I could not bear to make mistakes; my memory was retentive, my speech refined; friendship consoled me; pain, dishonour, ignorance I was able to avoid. Surely every part of such a creature calls for wonder and praise.

2. But all this is the bounty of my God and not my own; and all these capacities are good; and I am the sum of them. Truly, then, He who made me is good, and very good; and to Him will I give loud thanks for all the good that belonged to me, even as a boy. For my sin was just this, that I sought for pleasure, grandeur, reality, not in Him but in His creatures, myself and others, and thus fell headlong into sorrow, confusion, error. Thanks be unto Thee, O my God, my joy, my glory, and my confidence. Thanks be unto Thee for all Thy gifts; but do Thou keep them safe for me. For then Thou wilt keep me safe, and Thy gifts will increase and be perfected; and I shall be with Thee, for even my being is Thy gift.

BOOK II.

Going on to the next period of life
he tells, with heartfelt penitence,
of the first year of his youth,
which he spent in enforced idleness at home in lust and frolic;
and dwells with severe condemnation on a theft which he then
committed with his companions.

CHAPTER I

He recalls the age and the vices of Youth.

I DESIRE to record all my past vileness and the
carnal corruption of my soul: not that I love
the retrospect, but that I may love Thee, O my
God. For love of Thy love do I travel over again
in the bitterness of my self-examination my most
wicked ways; that Thou mayest be my joy, my
never-failing joy, my blessed and fearless joy; that
Thou mayest gather me again from the scattering
wherein I was torn limb from limb [1]; for, when
I turned from the One, I melted away into the
Many.

2. For in the time of youth I took my fill
passionately among the wild beasts, and I dared
to roam the woods and pursue my vagrant loves
beneath the shade; and my beauty consumed
away, and I was loathsome in Thy sight, pleasing
myself and desiring to please the eyes of men.

[1] Like Osiris in the fable. Turning from the One
is another phrase from Plotinus.

CHAPTER II

He inveighs against the fiery lust of Youth.

NOW what was it that gave me pleasure, save to love and to be loved? But I could not keep within the kingdom of light, where friendship binds soul to soul. From the quagmire of concupiscence, from the well of puberty, exhaled a mist which clouded and befogged my heart, so that I could not distinguish between the clear shining of affection and the darkness of lust. Both stormed confusedly within me, whirling my thoughtless youth over the precipices of desire, drowning it in the eddying pool of shame. Thy wrath lay heavy upon me, and I knew it not. I was deafened by the clanking of my chains, the punishment of the pride of my soul; and I wandered still farther from Thee, and Thou didst leave me to myself; the torrent of my fornications tossed and swelled and boiled and ran over, and Thou saidst nothing, O my late-found joy. Thou saidst nothing, and I went farther and farther away into the barren seed-plot of sorrow, full of proud dejection and restless discontent.

2. Could no one alleviate my distress, and turn to good account the fleeting charms of earthly beauty, setting a bound to their power, and forbidding the raging waves of my youth to pass the shore of married love. If the storm could not be wholly

calmed, I might have been content when I had
children, as Thy law ordains, O Lord, who
shapest even the offspring of our mortality, and
knowest how to train with gentle touch the
thorns shut out from Thy paradise; for Thy
omnipotence is not far from us, even when we
are far from Thee. Or at least I ought to have
heeded Thy voice from the clouds: " Nevertheless, such shall have trouble in the flesh; but I
spare you." And: " It is good for a man not
to touch a woman." And: " He that is un-
married thinketh of the things of the Lord, how
he may please the Lord; but he that is married
careth for the things of this world, how he may
please his wife." [1]

3. I should have hearkened diligently to these
words; I should have made myself an eunuch
for the kingdom of heaven's sake,[2] and waited
happily for Thy embrace. But, alas! I was
swept away from Thee by the boiling flood of
loose desires; I broke the bounds of Thy law,
yet could not escape Thy rod. For none can
escape. Thou wert ever near me, in wrathful
pity marring all my lawless delights with bitter
vexations, that I might learn to seek delights
without vexation, and that I should find none
such save Thee, O Lord,—save Thee, who shapest
our trouble by Thy precepts,[3] and smitest that
Thou mayst heal, and slayest lest we should die
away from Thee. Where was I, and how far was

[1] 1 Cor. vii. 1, 28, 32.   [2] Matt. xix. 12.
[3] Ps. xciv. 20, agreeing with xciii. 20 of the Vulgate.

I banished from the delights of Thy house in that sixteenth year of the age of my flesh, when the madness of lust, which human shame tolerates and Thy laws condemn, prostrated itself beneath the sceptre of the tyrant Wantonness? And my relatives took no heed to save me from my fall by marriage; their one care was that I should learn to make a telling speech.

CHAPTER III

Of his parents' resolve to send him away to the University.

DURING that year my studies were interrupted. I had been called home from Madaura, a neighbouring city, in which I had sojourned for instruction in literature and rhetoric, and my father, who was but a poor burgess of Thagaste, with a spirit beyond his purse, was saving up means for sending me to the more distant Carthage. All this I tell not to Thee, O God, but as in Thy sight to my race, the human race, or such small portion of it as may light upon this book. And why? That both I and my readers may consider out of what a depth we must needs cry unto Thee. And what is nearer to Thy ears than a penitent heart and a faithful life. Who did not then sing my father's praises, because out of a slender purse he provided for his son all that was needful for a residence at the

distant university? For even of those citizens
who were far wealthier than he, few took such
pains for the advancement of their children, and
yet this devoted father gave himself no concern
how I grew up towards Thee, or how chaste I
was, provided only that I became a man of culture—however destitute of Thy culture, O God,
who art the one true good Lord of Thy vineyard, my heart.

2. But while during that sixteenth year I
kept complete holiday in idleness enforced by
straitened means, and lived in the society of my
parents, the thorns of lust grew higher than my
head, and there was no hand to root them up.
Nay once, when my father saw me in the bath,
already bearing the first signs of turbulent youth,
he went and told my mother, bragging of his
hopes of grandchildren, running riot, like all this
world which loves the creature better than its
Creator, in the intoxication of a froward and
debased will. But in the bosom of my mother
Thou hadst already begun to build Thy temple,
and laid the foundations of Thy holy habitation;
while my father was still a catechumen, and that
but recently. And so she trembled with godly
fear, and, though I was not yet one of the faithful, dreaded lest I should fall into crooked ways,
wherein they walk who turn to Thee their backs
and not their faces.[1]

3. Alas, do I dare to say that Thou wast silent
while I strayed farther from Thee? Is it true
that Thou wast silent? Whose then were those

[1] Jer. ii. 27.

words which by the lips of my mother, Thy
faithful servant, Thou didst reiterate in my ears.
None of them reached my heart or shook my
purpose. I remember that in our private talks
she warned me with the deepest solicitude to flee
fornication, and above all never to corrupt a wife.
This seemed to me mere prudery, which a man
should be ashamed to heed. But it was Thy
voice, and I knew not; and I thought that Thou
wast silent and she spoke, while through her Thou
wast speaking, and in her Thou wast despised—
by me her son, the son of Thy handmaid, Thy
servant.[1] But I knew not, and plunged along so
blindly, that when I heard my fellows glorying
in their vices, and the vilest bragging loudest, I
was ashamed to be outstripped in disgrace, and
sinned not only for pleasure but for praise.

4. What but vice is blameworthy? Yet there
was I, making myself more vicious to escape
blame, and when I could not match the exploits
of that wicked crew, I made up tales, lest I
should be thought mean spirited or a poor sort of
fellow, because a little more innocent or a little
more chaste. Behold with what comrades I
roamed the streets of Babylon, and wallowed in
the gutters as in spices and precious ointments.
And in the very centre of that city of sin the
ghostly enemy trod me down and held me fast—
seducing me because I was easy to be seduced.
For even the mother of my flesh—who had fled
from the midst of Babylon,[2] yet was still limping
in the outskirts thereof—though she warned me

[1] Ps. cxvi. 16.　　　　[2] Jer. li. 6.

against unchastity, did not act upon what she
had heard her husband say about me, though she
saw that the danger was imminent and threatened
ruin in the future. She did not restrain my
passions within the bounds of lawful marriage, as
she should have done, if they could not be cut
away to the quick. And the reason was that she
was afraid, lest my hope should be hindered by
the drag of a wife, not the hope of eternal life,
which my mother possessed in Thee, but the
hope of literary distinction, which both my parents
coveted for me, my father because he thought
foolishly about me and hardly at all about Thee,
my mother because she considered that the usual
education would be not only no hindrance but a
positive help towards finding Thee. At anyrate
that is what I guess, when I recall, as well as I
can, the character of my parents. Moreover the
curb was slackened without regard to due severity,
and I was suffered to enjoy myself according to
my dissolute fancy So all around me was darkness, overclouding, O my God, the calm light of
Thy truth ; and my iniquity stood out as with
fatness.[1]

CHAPTER IV

*He confesses that with his companions he committed
a theft.*

THEFT certainly Thy law punishes, O Lord,
     as well as the law written in the hearts of
men, which not even sin can erase. For no thief

[1] Ps. lxxiii. 7, agreeing with lxxii. 7 of the Vulgate.

can abide another thief, even though the one be
rich and the other driven to crime by poverty.
And I resolved to steal, and did steal, not from
pressure of want or penury, but from scorn of
justice and the full-fed insolence of sin : For I
stole what I had in plenty, and much better.
What I wanted to enjoy was not the thing I
stole, but the actual sin of theft. There was a
pear tree just beyond our vineyard, laden with
fruit, but the pears were not tempting either to
the eye or to the taste. Till midnight we had
been rioting according to our pestilential habit,
about the open spaces of the town, and then we
marched off, a band of profligates, to shake and
strip the tree. We carried off huge loads, not to
feast upon but to throw to the hogs, though
perhaps we ate a few. And this we did merely
for the pleasure of doing wrong.

2. Look upon my heart, O my God, look
upon my heart, which Thou didst pity in the
depths of the abyss. Let my heart now tell
Thee what it was seeking then, how I was
selling my soul for nought, and there was no
cause for my wickedness but the wickedness
itself. It was ugly, and yet I loved it. I loved
my own destruction and my own transgression,
not the object of my transgression, but the transgression itself. A ruined soul was I, breaking
away from Thy starry heaven into outer
darkness, seeking from shame no profit but
shame.

CHAPTER V

That no man sins without a reason.

FOR there is something that pleases in all fair
things, in gold, in silver, and so forth. We
love to touch what is agreeable to the touch;
and for each of our senses there is a correspond-
ing quality in things which ministers to its
gratification. Earthly dignity, command, pre-
eminence have a glory of their own, from which
springs the lust of revenge; and yet for none of
these objects of desire may we leave Thee, O
Lord, or deviate from Thy commandment. So,
too, our life on earth has its peculiar charm, because it has a certain measure of dignity, a certain
affinity with all these lowest forms of beauty.

2. Friendship, too, is a sweet bond, because
it links together many souls in unity. All such
objects are the occasion of sin, because we incline
passionately towards these lowest goods, and lose
our hold of those that are better and higher, of
Thee, O Lord my God, and Thy truth and
Thy law. Even these meanest goods can give
delight, but not like Thine, O my God, who
madest all things, for in Thee doth the rightcous
delight, and Thou art the joy of the true of
heart.[1] And, therefore, when the judge is
enquiring why a crime was committed, he is
not satisfied until he has discovered the motive,

---

[1] Ps. lxiv. 10, differing from both the English and
the Vulgate.

in the desire of gaining or the fear of losing one of those goods which I call lowest. For they are beautiful, are shining; though, in comparison with higher goods and heavenly riches, they are poor and miserable things.

3. A man has committed murder. Why? He coveted his victim's wife or estate: he robbed for a living; he was afraid that the murdered man would rob him; he had been wronged, and thirsted for revenge. Would he have killed a man without reason for the mere satisfaction of shedding blood? It is incredible. We have, indeed, read of a savage madman who preferred gratuitous wickedness and cruelty, but Catiline had a reason to give—" Lest my hand or my will should get out of practice." [1] What did he mean? Why, that by the constant rehearsal of crime he might learn to sack Rome and seize upon office, power, and wealth; that he might fear no law and shrink from no peril, spurred on by his desperate poverty and his blood-stained conscience. Even Catiline then loved not wickedness in itself, but the prize of his wickedness.

CHAPTER VI

God is that true and perfect goodness, whereof temptation is the semblance.

ALAS, what was it then that I loved in thee, O my theft, thou midnight crime of my sixteenth year? How couldest thou be beauti-

[1] Sallust, *Catiline*, 16.

ful, seeing that thou wert a theft? Nay, art
thou anything that I should thus apostrophise
thee? Those pears that we stole were fair to
look upon, because they were Thy creatures, O
Thou Fairest of all and Creator of all, Thou
good God, Thou Chief Good, my true Good.
They were fair; but it was not for them that my
wretched soul lusted. I had plenty of better
pears; I gathered them only to steal. For I
flung them away when gathered, and tasted no
enjoyment but the wickedness, which gave me
all my delight. For, if I did eat one of those
pears, its flavour came from the sin.

2. And now, O Lord my God, I ask what it
was in theft that attracted me, and behold it has
no beauty. There is beauty in justice and wisdom, in reason and memory and the senses, and
even in the lowest acts of existence: there is
beauty in the stars, so glorious and lovely in their
orbs, in earth and sea, and the teeming swarms
that recruit the army of life; but theft has none
of these. No, not even that imperfect and
shadowy beauty which we see in vices that
allure. For pride apes loftiness, and Thou
alone art God exalted above all. Ambition
seeks honour and glory, and Thou art honourable above all, and glorious for ever. The
cruelty of powerful men would fain be feared;
yet whom should we fear except the one God,
whose power neither force nor fraud can baffle,
neither time nor place nor person can elude. The
caresses of the wanton would fain win love,
yet what caress is sweeter than Thy charity,

and what can we love so wholesome as Thy most shining and beautiful truth. Curiosity affects the pursuit of knowledge, but Thou knowest perfectly all things.

3. Ignorance, too, and even folly, shield themselves under the name of simplicity and innocence, because there is naught so simple as Thou, nought so innocent, since Thy words are adverse to the wicked man. And sloth seems to wish for peace, but what sure peace is there except the Lord? Luxury calls itself satisfaction and abundance, but Thou art the fullness of all things, and an unfailing treasure of incorruptible delight. Prodigality masquerades as generosity, but Thou art the bountiful Giver of all that is good. Avarice would possess many things, and Thou possessest all things. Envy wrangles about excellence, and what more excellent than Thou? Anger demands revenge, and Thou art the just avenger. Fear is appalled by the strange, the sudden; it guards against the perils that threaten the things it loves: but to Thee nothing is strange, nothing is sudden, none can separate from Thee what Thou lovest,[1] and there is no strong safety except in Thee. Melancholy pines over the loss of what it used to dote upon; it would be like Thee, from whom nought can be taken away.

4. Thus doth the soul play the harlot, when she turns away, and seeks outside Thee those joys which she can only find in their purity by

[1] Rom. viii. 9.

returning to Thee. He does but imitate Thee
badly who flies from Thee, and lifts up his horn
against Thee. Yet by that bad imitation he
proves that Thou art the Creator of all nature,
and that therefore it is not possible to fly from
Thee. What was it then that I loved in that
theft of mine? How was I imitating my Lord
in my bad and vicious way? Was there a
pleasure in defying the law, by fraud if not by
force, in playing at freedom in the prison-house,
in showing that I could do wrong with impunity,
which might seem a phantom of omnipotence?
Lo, such is the servant who runs away from his
Lord and attains a shadow. O what corruption!
What a horrible life, what a deep gulf of death!
To think that one should love what is forbidden,
just because it is forbidden!

CHAPTER VII.

*He thanks God for the forgiveness of his sins, and
for his preservation from many other sins.*

WHAT reward shall I give unto the Lord,[1]
because my soul feels no fear while my
memory recalls all this. I will love Thee,
O Lord, and thank Thee and confess unto Thy
Name; because Thou hast forgiven all that debt,
my evil and criminal deeds. To Thy grace,

[1] Ps. cxvi. 12, agreeing with Ps. cxv. 12 of the
Vulgate.

Thy pity, it is due that my sins melted away like ice. To Thy grace it is due that some evil I left undone. For what might I not have done, seeing that I loved even fruitless misdoing? And I confess that all is forgiven me, the evil that I did of my own accord, the evil that, through Thy guidance, I escaped.

2. What man, when he ponders his own infirmity, dare ascribe to his natural strength his chastity or his innocence? for then must he love Thee less as deeming the mercy, whereby Thou forgivest the sins of the penitent, less necessary. If any has been called by Thee, and has followed the call, and escaped those sins which I here record and confess, let him not scoff at me, because I was healed by that Physician, to whose goodness he owes it that he was never sick, or not so sick. Therefore, let him love Thee as much, yea, far more, because he sees that the same Hand, which rescued me from that cruel disease, guarded him from the approach of contagion.

CHAPTER VIII

What it was that attracted him in his Theft.

ALAS, what fruit had I formerly in those things,[1] which now I blush to recall; and especially in that theft, which I loved for the theft's sake. There was nothing else in it to

[1] Rom. vi. 21.

love, for the act itself was naught, and I was the more wretched on that very account. And yet I should not have done it by myself; that is what I recollect of my feelings at the time; I should certainly not have done it by myself. I loved then, also, the fellowship of my comrades. There was therefore something else besides the theft that attracted me? Nay, nothing else, because even that something is nothing.

2. Who can teach me, save He who shines upon my heart and penetrates its dark places— who can teach me the real meaning of this action, which I have been led thus to criticise and discuss and consider. For if I had cared for the pears I stole, if I had wanted to eat them, I might have sought to gratify my desire by committing that theft single-handed, if one could have done it; nor need I have increased the itching of my lust by rubbing like a hog against my mates. But there was no pleasure in the pears; the pleasure was in the act itself, in the companionship of sinners.

CHAPTER IX

The Infection of Evil Companionship.

NOW, what state of mind was that? None could have been viler; yet, alas, it was mine. But what was it? Who can understand what sins are? [1] Laughter tickled our hearts,

[1] Ps. xix. 12, agreeing with Ps. xviii. 23 of the Vulgate.

because people did not know what we were about, and would have been furious if they had known, and we succeeded in duping them. But then, why was I delighted with the act, because I did it in company? Is it because men rarely laugh alone? Rarely, it is true; yet sometimes a man will burst into laughter, when he is all by himself, if some odd thing strikes his eye or his fancy. But I myself should not—I certainly should not, if I was alone.

2. Lo, I lay before Thee, O Lord, the lively recollection of my soul. Alone I should never have committed that theft, wherein I sought not the thing stolen but the theft itself; I should assuredly have found no pleasure in doing it by myself, and I should not have done it. O unfriendly friendship! how strange was thy temptation! Out of sport and laughter came the desire to hurt, the eager wish to inflict a wrong—not for gain, nor even for revenge. Friends say: "Come, let us do it," and we are ashamed not to be shameless.

CHAPTER X

In God is all that is Good.

WHO can unravel this twisted and tangled skein. It is ugly: let me not think of it; let me not look at it. I crave for Thee, O Justice and Innocence, fair and lovely with heavenly light, and content that still aspires. With Thee is deep peace and life unruffled. Whoso enters into Thee enters into the joy of his Lord,[1] and shall not fear, and shall be perfect in the perfect. I fell away from Thee in my youth and went astray, O my God, far from Thy eternal rest, and I became unto myself a dry and barren land.

[1] Matt. xxv. 21.

BOOK III.

OF those years of his youth which he passed at Carthage in the study of literature. During this period he remembers how he was caught in the snare of impure love and fell into the heresy of the Manicheans. He discourses convincingly against the follies and the errors of that sect. He tells of his mother's tears, and of the promise which God gave her that he should be brought back to the truth.

CHAPTER I

How he was caught by love, which he pursued.

NEXT I went to Carthage, where debauchery bubbled around me like a frying-pan. I was not yet in love, but I loved the idea of love, and a deep-felt want made me hate myself, because I wanted less than I should. I sought something to love, loving as I say the idea of love, and hated the tranquil path, where there are no mouse-traps. For my inward man was famished for want of the inward food, Thyself, O my God, yet had I no appetite and felt no desire for the meat that perisheth not; and that not because I was full but because I was empty, and therefore disdained it. And thus my soul was sick and smitten with boils, and rushed desperately out of doors, seeking, like Job, to scrape itself with the things of sense. And yet, if these things of sense had had no soul, I could not have loved them. To love and to be loved was sweet to me, but sweeter still if I enjoyed the person that I loved.

2. And so I polluted the brook of friendship with the sewage of lust, and darkened its clear shining with smoke from hell, and yet, vile and disreputable as I was, my vanity was inordinate,

and I aspired to be known for my fashion and my wit. Also I plunged headlong into love, whose fetters I longed to wear. O my God, my Merciful One, how good Thou wast, and with what gall didst Thou embitter that cup of sweetness! For I was beloved; I attained my wish, the bondage of clandestine fruition, and proudly riveted round myself the chain of woe; then was I scourged with the red-hot iron rods of jealousy, suspicion, fears, anger, and quarrels.

CHAPTER II

His love for Tragedies.

THE stage also bewitched me, and its manifold pictures of my misery added fuel to my fire. Why is it that men desire to be saddened by the representation of tragic misfortunes, which they do not in the least desire to suffer? Yet the spectator does desire to be saddened by them, and the sadness is the very pleasure that he seeks. Surely this is wretched folly. For in proportion as a man's emotions are less wholesome, the more deeply is he moved by the passion of tragedy. Yet, when a man actually feels this passion, we call his state misery. When he participates in it by way of sympathy, we call it pity. But now what pity can there be for the puppets of the stage? No one expects the spectator to help them; he is only asked to shed a tear, and the more tears he sheds, the more he encourages the actor of an idle tale. And, if these old-world or imaginary calamities are acted in such a way that he cannot shed a tear at all, he goes home disgusted and critical; otherwise he keeps his seat, listens with all his ears, and enjoys the luxury of weeping. Do men then delight in tears and grief? Surely not, but in joy. Or shall we say that, though misery is painful, pity is pleasant, and that because there is no pity without grief, we seek grief for the sake of pity. So that the love of grief also runs from the brook of friendship.

2. But whither does that brook flow? Why does it fall into a torrent of boiling pitch, into seething pools of horrid lust, where by its own freewill it loses the crystal purity of its heavenly source, and is changed into the nature of that hateful flood? Are we then to banish Pity? By no means. There are times, then, when we must delight in grief. But beware of uncleanness, O my soul, for fear of my God and Guardian, the God of our fathers, who is to be praised and exalted above all for evermore.[1] Beware of uncleanness. For even now I am not pitiless. But while in the old days in the theatre I envied the lovers who enjoyed the forbidden fruits of love—though but in the mimicry of the stage—and grieved with a kind of pity when they were forced to part, and found the pity as pleasant as the joy, now I pity him who rejoices in his wicked success, and do not pity

---

[1] See Daniel iii. 52 (Vulgate).

him who has lost—what?—a ruinous pleasure, a miserable happiness.

3. Now certainly this is a juster pity, but there is no pleasure in its grief. For, though it is the approved office of charity to grieve over the wretched, a truly pitiful man would far rather see nothing to grieve over. One who really and sincerely pities, cannot want people to be wretched, in order that he may pity them, unless there is such a thing as malevolent benevolence, which is an impossibility. Grief then may sometimes be right, but never desirable. And this Thou teachest us, O Lord God, who lovest the soul with a love far purer than ours, and whose pity is diviner than ours, because it feels no grief. But who is sufficient for these things?[1] However, wretched man that I was, I loved sorrow in those days; I sought an outlet for pity in the fictitious woes of a dancer, and always that part liked me best which wrung tears from my eyes. What wonder, if the lost and wilful sheep was taken by the murrain? Thence came my delight in troubles—not such as pierce the heart, for I would not for the world have suffered what I was so eager to behold—but idle tales which glance upon the surface—yet they tore my flesh like claws, and left behind them an angry swelling and a festering sore. Is such a life worth calling life, O my God?

[1] 2 Cor. ii. 16

CHAPTER III

*In the Rhetoric School he took no part in the
doings of the Wreckers.*

AND always Thy faithful mercy hovered over
me from afar. O in what wickednesses
did I consume away! How did I follow my
profane Curiosity, till it led me into the very
depths of unbelief, into the deceitful worship of
devils to whom my misdeeds were a sacrifice!
And always Thou wast scourging me. I was
not afraid to think of my lust, and plan a scheme
for securing the deadly fruit of sin, even within
the walls of Thy church during the celebration of
Thy mysteries. For this Thou didst chastise
me with heavy penalties, yet not as my fault
deserved, O my God, my surpassing Mercy, my
Refuge from the awful tormentors among whom I
wandered with stubborn neck, fleeing farther
and farther from Thee, loving my own ways not
Thine, loving a runagate freedom.

2. My studies also, liberal studies they were
called, drew me to look towards the Law Courts
and aspire to success at the bar, where the craftiest
is the most honourable. Such is the blindness of
men, who ever glory in their blindness. And
now I had reached the top of the school of
rhetoric. Proud enough I was, and puffed up
with conceit, yet far quieter than I had been, O
Lord, Thou knowest. I would take no part at

all in the wild doings of the Wreckers, a cruel and devilish name, which was looked upon as the stamp of the best set. I lived amongst them, feeling a kind of impudent shame, because I could not keep pace with them. I went about with them, and of some of them I made friends; yet I always disliked their way of going on, their "wreckings," their wanton attacks upon the shyness of freshmen, and the unprovoked affronts with which they carried on their malignant amusement. Nothing could be more like the conduct of devils, and what name could be fitter for them than Wreckers? They themselves were wrecked and broken to begin with, and the lying spirits were cozening and seducing them, while they were finding delight in flouting and deceiving others.

CHAPTER IV

The Hortensius of Cicero roused in him a great love of Philosophy.

AMONG such comrades in those years of in-discretion, I was studying books of rhetoric, wherein I desired to excel, seeking through the joys of vanity a flashy and reprobate success, and in the usual course I had entered upon a book by one Cicero whose tongue all men admire, though not his heart. It was the *Hortensius*, a treatise in which he extols the study of philosophy. That book changed my mind, changed my very prayers to Thee, O Lord, and altered my wishes and aspirations. From that moment vain hopes ceased to charm, and with a strange and heartfelt passion I began to long for the immortality of wisdom. Thenceforth began my upward way, and my return towards Thee. For I did not apply that book to the sharpening of my tongue, an accomplishment which it seemed hard to purchase at my mother's cost—for I was in my nineteenth year and my father had died two years before—I did not, I say, apply it to the sharpening of my tongue, for what the book itself commended was not the style but the substance of speech.

2. How did I burn, O my God, how did I burn to soar away from earth to Thee; yet I knew not what Thou wast doing to me. For wisdom is Thine. The love of wisdom with which those pages inspired me is called in Greek "philosophy." There are some who mislead by philosophy, tricking out their own errors with a high, attractive and honourable title, and in this book Cicero censures and confutes nearly all these erroneous teachers of his own or earlier times. How distinctly does he preach the wholesome admonition, which Thy Spirit gives by the mouth of Thy good and pious servant: " Beware lest any man spoil you through philosophy and vain deceit, after the tradition of men, after the rudiments of the world and not after Christ. For in Him dwelleth all the fullness of the Godhead bodily." [1]

[1] Col. ii. 8, 9.

3. At that time, Thou knowest O Light of my heart, these words of the Apostle were not yet known to me; yet the one point that came home to me in Cicero's book was the advice not to run after this school or that, but to love, and seek, and pursue, and clasp, and never let go Wisdom herself, wherever I found her. I was strongly moved, and kindled, and inflamed by these words; and one thing only damped my zeal, that the Name of Christ was not mentioned there. For this Name, according to Thy loving-kindness, O Lord, this Name of my Saviour, Thy Son, my infant heart had sucked in with my mother's milk, and there it still was, hidden safe away. So that any book which did not use that Name —cultivated, polished, profound as it might be— could not wholly master me.

CHAPTER V

He disdained sacred Scripture because of its style.

AND so I determined to read the sacred Scriptures, and find out what they were like. And behold I found a thing not known to the proud, nor laid open to children, but lowly in mien, lofty in operation, and veiled in mysteries. I was not such that I could enter into it, or bow my head at its approach. For I did not feel what I have just described, when first I read the Scriptures. They seemed to me to be far inferior to the dignity of Tully. My extravagance disliked their self-restraint, and my eye could not pierce their hidden depths. In truth it is the nature of that Book to grow with the growth of the babe. But I disdained to be a babe, and in my swelling pride fancied that I was grown-up.

CHAPTER VI

How he was caught by the Manichees.

AND so I fell among a sort of men vain and brain-sick, carnal and verbose, in whose mouths were snares of the Devil and lime for silly birds, made up of the syllables of Thy Name, and that of our Lord Jesus Christ, and that of the Paraclete our Comforter, the Holy Ghost. These Names were never off their lips; the sound was there, and the movement of the tongue, but the heart within was void of truth. "The Truth, the Truth," they were always saying, and often said to me, but it was not in them [1]; they taught lies, not only of Thee who art the true Truth, but of the elements of this world, Thy creatures. But, indeed, I ought not to have heeded philosophers, even though they spoke truth about Thy works: I ought to have passed them by for love of Thee, my Father, supremely good, Thou Fairness of all that is fair. O

[1] 1 John ii. 4.

G

Truth, Truth, how did the inmost marrow of my soul sigh for Thee even then, while those word-mongers were ringing the changes on Thy name in all those ponderous tomes! These were the dainty dishes wherein, when I was hungering for Thee, they served up to me the sun and moon, beautiful works indeed, but Thy works, not Thyself nor even Thy first works. For Thy spiritual world came before these material creatures, bright and heavenly though they be.

2. I hungered and thirsted not even for those, Thy first works, but for Thee, O Truth, in whom is no variableness, neither shadow of turning,[1] yet still they set before me in those dainty dishes a banquet of delusions. Far better were it to love the sun we see (which to our eyes, at any rate, is real) than these fictions of a mind deceived by the eyes. And yet I fed on them because I took them for Thee, but not with appetite, because I could not find in them Thy savour. For Thou wast not those fictions, nor did they nourish, nay, they starved me. How like is food in dreams to real food! yet the dreamer is not fed, for it is a dream. But these meats were not like Thee in any way, as Thou didst warn me even then; for they were material notions, imaginary things, far less certain than the real things, which we see with our natural eyes, in earth or sky. These the birds and beasts see as well as we; and they are far more real than those creatures of the imagination. And again, those imaginations are far more

[1] James i. 17.

real than the infinite series of sublime nonentities which we build upon them. However, with these empty husks was I then fed, yet not fed.

3. But Thou, my Love, for whom I faint that I may be made strong, art neither these bodies which we see, though they be in heaven, nor those which we see not, for Thou art their Creator, nor dost Thou count them among Thy chiefest works. How far art Thou, then, from those notions that I believed in, notions of bodies which do not exist at all. For our abstract conceptions of bodies which do exist are more certain than they, and the bodies themselves are more certain still, yet Thou art none of these. Thou art not even the soul, which is the life of bodies, so that the life of bodies is better and more certain than the bodies themselves. But Thou art the life of souls, the life of lives, having life in Thyself, and never changest, O Life of my soul. Where wast Thou then? How far away from me? while I was banished far away from Thee, deprived even of the husks of the swine which I was feeding with husks. For the fables of the grammarian and the poet were far better than this deceitful stuff. Beyond a doubt verses and songs about Medea's flight through the air are more profitable than the five elements variously transformed because of the five caves of darkness, which have no existence, and slay him that believes in them. From verses and songs I can find real nutriment, and, as for Medea and her flight, even if I sang about it, I did not maintain that it was true. And when others sang about

it, I did not believe them.   But these absurdities
I did believe.

4. Alas! alas! by what steps was I brought
down to the depths of hell! [1] toiling and chafing
for lack of truth, and all, O my God (for unto
Thee do I confess it, who hadst pity on me,
even when I did not confess), all because I was
seeking for Thee by the carnal senses, and not
by that intelligence in which Thou madest me
superior to the beasts.   But Thou wast lower
than my lowest depth and higher than my highest
height.   And so I happened upon that brazen
and witless woman of whom Solomon speaks in
his parable, sitting on a chair at the entrance of
the door, and crying: "Eat gladly of hidden
bread and drink sweet stolen water." [2]   She corrupted me because she found me rambling abroad
in the lust of the eye, and ruminating such food
as I had procured for myself thereby.

CHAPTER VII

*The absurdity of the Manichean doctrine,
which he professed.*

FOR, knowing not the true Being, I was so
shaken by quips and quiddities that I had
no answer for these silly deceivers when they
asked me what is the origin of evil? whether

[1] Prov. ix. 18.
[2] Prov. ix. 13-17.   Differing from both the English
and the Vulgate.

God is limited by a bodily form? whether he has hair and nails? whether polygamists, homicides, offerers of bloody sacrifices, can be regarded as righteous men? These doubts confused my ignorance; I turned my back on truth and thought I was looking for it, because I did not know that evil is the privation of good and next door to non-existence. How could I see this, when my eye could see nothing but bodies, and my mind nothing but materialised ideas?

2. I did not understand that God is a spirit,[1] who has no parts that can be measured, whose being is not a bulk, because bulk is less in the part than in the whole, and, even if it be infinite, is less in some definite portion than in its infinity, and cannot be wholly everywhere like God, who is spirit. And I had not the least conception in what we are like God, or whether Scripture was right in saying that we are in the image of God.[2] Nor did I know the true inner righteousness, which judges not conventionally but by the upright law of Almighty God, whereby the customs of countries and times are adapted to the countries and the times, though the law is the same everywhere and always. I did not see that by this law Abraham and Isaac and Jacob and Moses and David and all who are praised by the mouth of God were righteous; though they were counted unrighteous by foolish men, judging by man's day,[3] and measuring the morality of the whole human race by the petty rule of their own morality, just as if one, who knew nothing about

[1] John iv. 24.   [2] Gen. i. 27.   [3] 1 Cor. iv. 3.

armour, should fasten a greave on his head and shoe his foot with a helmet, and then complain because they do not fit; or as if, when a holiday has been proclaimed for the afternoon, he should make a disturbance because he may not open his shop after twelve o'clock, though it was lawful in the morning; or as if in some great household, having discovered that one slave was allowed to handle things which the butler might not touch, or that things might be done in the stable which were forbidden in the dining room, he should make angry complaints, that in one house and in one family all have not the same office at the same time.

3. Such are they who are indignant, when they hear that some things were lawful for the righteous in old times, which are not permitted now; or that God for temporary reasons gave the ancients one commandment, us another, though we both obey the same righteousness; or when they see that in one man, in one day, in one house, different offices suit different members, that what was right just now is not right when the clock has struck, that what is done, nay, must be done, in one room is properly forbidden and punished in another. Is justice then capricious or changeable? No, but the times, over which justice presides, do not run evenly, because they are times. So men, whose days upon earth are few, quarrel with the past and accept the present, because they cannot actually see the connection between the laws that governed ages and nations of old and those that are now in operation; while they can see individuals, days, houses, in which

different things at different moments are suitable
to different members, parts, or persons.

4. All these things I neither knew nor considered; they forced themselves upon my eyes,
but I could not see them. I wrote poems, in
which I was not allowed to put any foot I
pleased wherever I liked; each metre had its
own regulations, and, even in the same line, the
same foot would not suit all places. Yet the
art of poetry did not make its principles to suit
the case, but comprised all in one. Still I did
not perceive that justice, which those good and
holy men obeyed, comprises all in one in a far
more excellent and admirable way; that, without changing in any degree, it yet gives out its
precepts, not all at once, but with due respect
to the changes of the times. And in my blindness I condemned the holy patriarchs; though
they not only regulated the present by the command and inspiration of God, but moreover foretold the future as God revealed it unto them.

CHAPTER VIII

*Against the Manicheans he shows what vices and
what crimes are always detestable.*

CAN it ever or anywhere be wrong to love
God with all thy heart and all thy soul
and all thy mind, and thy neighbour as thyself? [1]
Crimes therefore which are offences against

[1] Matt. xxii. 37.

nature are everywhere and always abominable and punishable. Such were those of the people of Sodom. If all nations were to do the like, they would stand guilty in the same degree before the divine law, because it did not so make men that they should treat one another thus. Even the fellowship ordained between us and God is broken, when that nature of which He is author is polluted by abnormal lust. But crimes, which are offences against the customs of man, are to be avoided out of respect for these customs, which vary. The rule is, that neither native nor foreigner should wantonly break the mutual compact established by the manners or the laws of any state or nation. Because it is unnatural for the part to rebel against the whole, of which it is a part.

2. But, when God directs anything to be done against the law or compact of any state, even if it has never been done there, it is to be done; if it were discontinued, it is to be resumed; if it had never been ordered, it is to be ordered. For if it is lawful for a king in his own kingdom to command what neither he himself nor any of his predecessors had before commanded, and obedience in such a case is not against the commonweal, nay, disobedience is against the commonweal— for the general compact of human society is that they should obey their prince—how much more ought we to obey God, the ruler of all created things, without hesitation, in all that He directs. For as in the hierarchy of human authority, the lesser power obeys the greater, so all are sub-

ordinate to God. The same rule holds in crimes, where there is a desire to cause damage, either by way of insult or by way of injury, and either may be inflicted for the sake of revenge, as between enemies, or for the sake of gain, as when a robber plunders a traveller, or to avoid harm, or to one who is feared, or out of envy, as by the unlucky against the fortunate, or by the prosperous against a present or prospective rival, or from pure delight in cruelty, as is the case with the spectators at a gladiatorial show, and with all who mock and insult others. These are the shoots of iniquity, which sprout up from the desire of pre-eminence, or of strong emotion of sight or feeling, or from one or two or all of them ; and thus men lead ill lives, in defiance of the three and the seven,[1] the harp of ten strings,[2] Thy Decalogue, O God, Thou highest and sweetest.

3. But what vices, what crimes are offences against Thee, since Thou canst neither be polluted nor injured ? Yet Thou dost punish men's offences against Thee, because while they sin against Thee they wrong their own souls, and their iniquity gives itself the lie,[3] either by ruining or perverting the nature which Thou didst create and ordain, or in things lawful, by excess,

[1] St Augustine divides the Decalogue, according to Latin usage, into *three* commandments concerning our duty to God, and *seven* concerning our duty to our neighbours.

[2] Ps. cxliv. 9.

[3] Ps. xxvii. 12 agreeing with Ps. xviii. 13-14 of the Vulgate.

or in things not lawful, by burning for that use which is against nature;[1] or again Thou dost hold them guilty, because in will and word they rebel against Thee and kick against the pricks,[2] or because, following the guidance of their own likings or dislikings, they take pleasure in coteries or schisms, and boldly renounce their allegiance to society at large.

4. Such is the consequence, when Thou art abandoned, who art the Fount of Life, the one true Creator and ruler of the whole world, when in the pride of independence men set their hearts on a part instead of the whole, on some one false good. So meekness and piety are the way back to Thee, and Thou dost cleanse us from our evil habits, forgiving the sins that are confessed, hearing the sighs of the prisoner,[3] breaking the chains that we forged for ourselves —if only we lift no more against Thee the horns of a fancied liberty, risking our all on the chance of more, loving our own good more than Thee, the Good of all.

CHAPTER IX

The difference between one sin and another, and between the judgment of God and of man.

BUT among vices and crimes and all the host of transgressions, some sins are scholars' faults. These the judicious condemn by the rule of perfection, yet praise in hope of fruit, because

[1] Rom. i. 26.   [2] Acts ix. 5.   [3] Ps. cii. 20.

they may be compared to the green blade, giving
promise of the full ear. Some actions, again, re-
semble a vice or a crime, yet are not sins, because
they offend neither against Thee, our Lord God,
nor against the social bond : as, for instance,
there are kinds of property, suitable to a given
period of time, though not to others, which men
may acquire without clear presumption of un-
lawful greed ; there are kinds of punishment
which, barbarous as they may be, if inflicted by
a constituted authority for the sake of correction,
need not imply a delight in cruelty. Many
actions, which men might censure, are approved
by Thy testimony, and many, which men have
applauded, are condemned by Thee ; because the
relation of the deed to the motive of the agent
and the inscrutable conditions of the time must
often vary.

2. But when Thou dost of a sudden command some strange and unexpected act, though
Thou hast beforetime forbidden it—though Thou
dost for the time conceal the reason of the command—though it be against the compact of a
particular society of men—who can doubt that
it ought to be done, since that society alone is
rightly ordered which is in obedience to Thee ?
But blessed are they who know that Thou
hast commanded. For whatsoever Thy
servants do, is done either to supply what is
necessary for the present, or to foreshow things
to come.

CHAPTER X

Absurd Manichean belief about Vegetable Life.

AT that time I knew not this, and mocked at Thy holy servants and prophets. Yet what was the result, except that Thou didst mock at me? Step by step I was drawn on to such a pitch of absurdity as to believe that a fig weeps when it is plucked, and that the mother tree weeps for the fig with milky tears. Yet, if a saint ate and digested that fig, provided that some one else had committed the sin of plucking it, he would breathe forth angels, yes, actual particles of God, as he sighed and gasped in prayer. And these particles of the highest and true God would have remained imprisoned in the fruit, unless they had been set free by the teeth and the gastric juices of an elect saint. And I believed, wretched man that I was, that the fruits of earth deserve more pity than man, for whose use they grow. For if a hungry man, who was not a Manichee, had begged for a mouthful, I should have thought it a deadly sin to give him one.

CHAPTER XI

The sorrow and the dream of Monnica about Augustine.

AND Thou didst send forth Thy hand from above,[1] and save my soul from this depth of darkness, in answer to the tears of my mother,

[1] Ps. cxliv. 7.

Thy faithful one, for she wept for my errors
mere bitterly than most mothers for the death of
their offspring. For, in the light of the faith
and the spirit which Thou gavest her, she saw
that I was dead. And Thou didst hear her, O
Lord, Thou didst hear her, and despisedest not
the tears with which she watered the ground as
she knelt in prayer. Thou didst hear her ; or
whence came that consoling dream, in consequence of which she allowed me to live with her
and eat at the same table, after she had forbidden
me to do so in horror at my blasphemous errors ?
She dreamed that she was weeping and lamenting,
with her feet planted on a wooden rule, when she
saw coming towards her a radiant youth, who
smiled upon her cheerfully. He asked the
reason of her sorrow and her daily tears (for the
sake, as is the angel's wont, of teaching not of
learning), and when she told him she was bewail-
ing my perdition, he bade her be of good comfort,
look and see, for where she was, there was I also.
She looked, and saw me standing by her side on
the same rule. Now whence was this, but that
Thy ear was listening to her heart?

2. O Thou Almighty Goodness, who carest
for each one of us, as if Thou caredst for him
alone, and for all as if they were each alone !
How came this too, that when she had told me
her dream, and I tried to make it mean that she
need not despair, because she would one day be
what I was, she answered without a moment's
hesitation : "No, he did not say where he is you
will be, but where you are he will be." I con-

fess to Thee, O Lord, that to the best of my recollection (and I have often spoken about it), I was far more impressed by Thy answer delivered by my mother, and by the quickness of the retort—for she was not disturbed by my plausible interpretation, and saw in an instant what was plain enough, though I did not see it before she spoke—than by the dream itself, wherein the long deferred joy of that religious woman was foretold for the consolation of her present distress.

3. For still, during the space of almost nine years, I wallowed in the slime and the darkness of that pit of error, often trying to rise, but always falling deeper. All that time that chaste, devout and sober widow (such are dear to Thee) with growing hope, but unremitted sighs and tears, ceased not at all her hours of devotion to lament unto Thee for me. Lo, her prayers entered into Thy sight,[1] and yet Thou didst suffer me still to welter in that darkness.

CHAPTER XII

What answer Monnica received about the conversion of her son.

ANOTHER answer Thou didst give in the meanwhile, which I call to mind, though I pass over much, because I hasten on to more pressing confessions, and much I do not re-

[1] Ps. lxxxviii, 2 agreeing with Ps. lxxxvii. of the Vulgate.

member. Thou gavest another by the mouth of
Thy priest, a bishop brought up in Thy church
and deeply read in Thy books. My mother had
begged him to speak with me, to refute my errors,
unteach me evil and teach me good, and this it was
his wont to do, when he found apt listeners.
But he refused, and wisely, as I afterwards
came to see. For, said he, I was as yet unwilling to learn, because I was puffed up with the
novelty of that heresy, and had already perplexed
many simple persons with my sophisms, as she
had told him. "Leave him where he is," he
added, "only pray the Lord for him; he will
learn by his own reading, what an error and an
impiety it is."

2. At the same time he told her that he himself, when a child, had been given up by his
misguided mother to the Manichees, and had not
only read but copied out nearly all their books,
but that gradually, without discussion or refutation,
he had come to see that the sect was to be
abandoned, and that he had abandoned it accord-
ingly. But she would not be persuaded, and
pressed him the more with entreaties and tears to
see and reason with me, till at last he took
umbrage and cried, "Go, and God be with you;
it cannot be that the son of these tears should be
lost." These words, as she often told me afterwards, she accepted as a voice from heaven.

BOOK IV.

Hᴇ confesses with shame that for
nine years he adhered to the
Manichean sect, and seduced
others into the same errors, and,
taking occasion from the death of
a friend, which he had lamented
with excessive grief, he enlarges
upon the difference between true
and false Friendship. He notices
his own books on the Beautiful
and Fit, and tells how easily he
understood without a teacher the
Categories of Aristotle and the
text-books of the liberal arts in
the twentieth year of his age.

H

CHAPTER I

How long and in what manner he misled others.

DURING this space of nine years, from the nineteenth to the twenty-eighth year of my age, I was misled and misleader, deceived and deceiver in various fond desires, openly by means of those arts and accomplishments which men call liberal, secretly in the cause of a false religion—now proud, now superstitious, always naught. Education drew me to follow the toys that men call fame, applause in the theatre, prize poems, contests for crowns of hay, the follies of the stage, all the riot of passion. Religion taught me to seek purification from the defilements of the flesh by supplying food to those who were called "elect saints," in order that, in the laboratory of their paunches, they might manufacture angels and gods for my redemption. These were my pursuits; these things I did with my friends, deceived by me and with me.

2. Let the proud make a mock of me, and those who have not yet, for their soul's health, been stricken down and bruised by Thee, O my God; yet will I confess unto Thee my shame for Thy glory. Have patience with me

I beseech Thee, and suffer me to retrace in memory the mazes of my bygone wanderings, and to offer unto Thee the sacrifice of jubilation.[1] For without Thee what am I unto myself but a guide to ruin? Or what am I even when it is well with me but an infant suckled on Thy milk, or feeding on Thee, the meat that perisheth not?[2] Or what is any man since he is but man? Yes, let the strong and the mighty make a mock of me; yet will I the weak and needy confess unto Thee.[3]

CHAPTER II

He became rhetoric professor, took a concubine, and looked upon augury with contempt.

IN those years I became a teacher of rhetoric, and, because I could not conquer my greed, I sold the art of conquering in the strife of words. Yet (O Lord Thou knowest) I preferred honest scholars, as men count honesty, and guilelessly I taught them guile, not that they should ruin the innocent, but that sometimes they might save the guilty. And Thou, O God, sawest me from afar off stumbling on that slippery ground, and, amid all my smoke, there was, withal, some little spark of fidelity in my diligence towards my pupils, though they

[1] Ps. cxvi. 17, differing both from the English and the Vulgate.
[2] John vi. 27.   [3] Ps. lxxiv. 21.

loved vanity and sought after leasing.[1] In those years I lived with one not joined to me in lawful wedlock, upon whom my vagabond foolish passion had settled, yet with but one, and I was faithful to her. Then did I learn by my own experience the difference between the chaste alliance of marriage, contracted in hope of children, and the licentious bargain of carnality, wherein the parents desire no children, though, when once they are born, they cannot help loving them.

2. I remember also that, when I had resolved to compete for a prize for verses to be recited in the theatre, an augur sent to ask me what I would give to win. But I so heartily detested those vile mysteries that I answered, "If it were a crown of immortal gold, not a fly should be sacrificed to buy my victory." He would have killed living creatures in sacrifice, and by these offerings solicited his demons to help me. But even this sin I did not reject out of love for Thee, O God of my heart. For how could I love Thee, when I could conceive of nothing better than a shining kind of body. When the soul sighs after such foolish fancies, does it not play the harlot against Thee, and trust in falsehood, and feed the winds?[2] Forsooth, I would not let an augur offer sacrifice on my behalf to demons; while I was offering myself as a sacrifice to them by my Manichean superstition. For we feed the winds when we feed the demons; that is to say, when by our errors we give them food for laughter and mockery.

[1] Ps. iv. 2.   [2] Hosea xii. 7.

CHAPTER III

*How his inclination to astrology was corrected by
a wise old physician.*

AND so I did not think it at all necessary to
abstain from consulting those astronomers
who are called mathematicians, on the ground
that they neither offer sacrifice nor pray to any
spirit for the purpose of divination. Yet this
also is rightly forbidden and condemned by true
Christian piety. For it is a good thing to confess unto Thee, O Lord, and to say " Have
mercy on me ; heal my soul for I have sinned
against Thee," and not to abuse Thy kindness
for a license to sin, but remember what the Lord
said : " Behold thou art made whole; sin no
more lest a worse thing happen unto thee." [1]
This wholeness or healthiness the astrologer
labours to destroy, saying, " From the sky comes
the inevitable cause of thy sin," or " Venus did
this or Saturn or Mars " ; so that man, who is
but flesh and blood and proud corruption, should
be exempt from guilt, and all the blame for his
misdeeds should fall on the creator and ruler of
the sky and the stars. And who is He but our
God, the sweetness and fountain of all righteousness, who will requite to every man according to
his works,[2] and despiseth not the humble and
contrite heart.[3]

[1] John v. 14.   [2] Rom. ii. 6.   [3] Ps. li. 7.

2. There was at that time a man of great wisdom,[1] deservedly famous for his skill in the art of medicine. He happened to be proconsul, and with his own hand had placed upon my head the crown that I had won in the theatrical competition. Alas, my head was disordered, but he was not the physician who could cure it. For of that disease Thou art the only healer, who resistest the proud and givest grace unto the humble.[2] Yet, even by that aged man, Thou didst help me, and work towards the curing of my soul. For I became acquainted with him, and took great delight in his conversation, which from the pregnancy of his judgment was agreeable and weighty, though he pretended to no polish of language. He gathered from my talk that I studied books of astrology, and thereupon admonished me with most fatherly kindness to throw them aside, and waste no more valuable time on such absurdities. He told me that he himself had learned astrology, when a young man, with the intention of gaining a livelihood by that profession, that, as he could understand Hippocrates, I must not suppose that he could not understand those books; but that he had given them up and taken to medicine, because he found them to be wholly false, and could not condescend, being a serious man, to earn his bread by deception. "But you," he added, "have the means of support in your rhetoric; you study these delusions out of curiosity, not

[1] His name, Vindicianus, is given below, vii. 6.
[2] 1 Peter v. 5.

from need, and therefore should more readily credit what I tell you about an art which I mastered with the thoroughness of one who hoped to get a living by it.''

3. When I asked him how then it happened that the predictions of astrologers often proved true, he replied, as well he might, " Because of the power of chance, which runs through all nature. Thus a man will seek an oracle in the pages of a poet,[1] who is singing and thinking about something quite different, and often a verse will come out quite pat to the business in hand. Yet it is no wonder that from a human soul, prompted unconsciously by an instinct from above, a word should drop, by chance not by art, with some sort of bearing upon the purpose of the enquirer.'' This light Thou didst give me from him, or through him, and didst fix in my memory doubts, which I might afterwards verify for myself. But at that time neither he nor my dear Nebridius, a young man of great goodness and prudence, who laughed at the whole system of divination, could persuade me to give it up, because I thought the weight of authority was on the other side, and because as yet I had not found the clear and certain proof I wanted, that, when an astrologer did speak the truth, he was guided by chance, not by skill, in reading the stars.

[1] Augustine is alluding to the *Sortes Virgilianae.* See the Article on *Sortilegy* in the *Dictionary of Christian Antiquities.*

CHAPTER IV

Of the sickness and death of a friend, whom he had corrupted with his own errors, and of his grief at that death.

IN those years, soon after I began to be a teacher in my native town of Thagaste, I had gained a friend endeared to me by parity of age, for we were both in the opening flower of life, and still more by similarity of pursuits. We had grown up as boys together; we had gone to the same school, and shared the same games. Yet neither as boy nor as youth was he a friend in the true sense of friendship; for friendship is not true, unless Thou dost form the bond between them who cleave to Thee with that love which is shed abroad in our hearts, by the Holy Ghost which is given to us.[1] Yet it was a sweet relation, cemented by zeal for common studies. I had even succeeded in drawing him away from the true faith for he was a believer, but not deeply nor experimentally, being but a youth, into those superstitious and mischievous fables, which gave my mother such grief on my account. And so he was wandering with me in error, and my soul could not live without him. And now, lo, pressing hard upon the flight of Thy runaway slaves, thou God of vengeance[2] and fountain of pity, who dost convert us to Thyself in ways so

[1] Rom. v. 5. [2] Ps. xciv. 1.

wonderful—lo, Thou didst take him away from this life, when we had scarcely completed one whole year in a friendship dear to me above all the joys of my life at that time.

2. Who can count up all Thy praises,[1] even those which he has experienced in himself alone ? What was it that Thou didst then, O my God, and how inscrutable is the depth of Thy judgments ![2] He was sick of a fever, and lay long unconscious in a deadly sweat. All hope being at an end, he was baptised, while yet unconscious, nor did I care, for I felt sure that his soul would retain what he had learned from me, and that it mattered little what was done to his insensible body. Yet it turned out quite otherwise, for he was newborn and made whole. As soon as I could have speech with him—and that was as soon as he could bear it, for I never left his side, and we were bound up in one another— I ventured a jest, thinking that he would jest too, about the baptism which he had received, when he could neither think nor feel. But by this time he had been told of his baptism. He shrank from me as from an enemy, and, with a wonderful new-found courage, warned me never to speak so to him again, if I wished to remain his friend.

3. I was so astounded and confused that I said no more, resolving to wait till he should regain his strength, when I would tell him frankly what I thought. But he was torn away from my madness, that he might be preserved in Thy king-

[1] Ps. cvi. 2.   [2] Ps. xxxvi. 6.

dom for my consolation.   A few days afterwards,
while I was away, the fever returned and he died.
This sorrow fell like darkness on my heart, and
wherever I looked I saw nothing but death.
My country became a torture, my father's house
a misery.   All the pleasures, that I had shared
with him, turned into hideous anguish now that
he was gone.   My eyes sought for him everywhere, and found him not.   I hated the familiar
scenes, because he was not there, and they could
no more cry to me " Lo ! he will come," as
they used, when he was absent but alive.   I
became a riddle to myself, and questioned my
soul why she was so heavy and disquieted me so
sorely,[1] and I could find no answer.   And if I
said " Have hope in God," she rightly refused
to listen, because the darling, whom she had lost,
was better and more real than the phantom in
whom I bade her hope.   Tears were my only
comfort, and took my friend's place in my heart's
desire.

CHAPTER V

Why tears are sweet to the wretched.

AND now, O Lord, all this sorrow is long
since past, and time has healed my wound.
May I learn from Thee, who art Truth, may I
lay the ear of my heart to Thy lips, that Thou
mayest whisper to me why tears are sweet to the

[1] Ps. xliii. 5.

sorrowful ? Or must I think that, though Thou art everywhere, Thou hast put far away from Thee all our woes ? Thou remainest self-contained ; we toss upon the tide of experience ; yet, unless thou couldst hear our lamentations, our hope would wholly vanish. How is it then that we cull from the bitterness of life the sweet fruits of groans and tears, of sighs and complaints ? Is this the sweetness, that we hope that Thou dost hear ? It is so in prayers, because in them we yearn to reach Thee. But is it true also of our regrets, and of such grief as then overwhelmed me ? Certainly I had no hope that he would return to me, nor did I pray for this even while I wept ; I simply grieved and mourned. For I was wretched, and I had lost my joy. Or is weeping mere bitterness, and does it please us only because we loathe the things that once we delighted in, and only so long as we loathe them ?

CHAPTER VI

What grief he felt at the death of his friend.

BUT why do I speak thus ? For it is no time for solving doubts, when I am confessing unto Thee. I was wretched, and every one is wretched so long as he is fettered by love of the perishable ; torn by the grief of parting the soul begins to feel the wretchedness, which was there before the parting came. So was I at that time ;

bitterly did I weep, and I found comfort in bitterness. Thus I was wretched, and my wretched life was dearer to me than my friend had been. Gladly as I would have changed it, I would rather have been deprived of my friend than of my grief. The story (or is it a fable?) tells how Orestes and Pylades would cheerfully have died for one another, or together, because separation was to them worse than death. But I doubt whether I could have sacrificed myself for him. A strange feeling had sprung up in me, pointing in quite a different direction; I was sick of living, yet afraid to die. I suppose that the intensity of my love made death, which had robbed me of him, seem hateful and dreadful, like some horrid enemy; and I thought that it must soon destroy all men, because it had slain him. This was my frame of mind; I remember it quite distinctly.

2. Yes, I remember it. Behold my heart, O my God; behold my secret thoughts, O my Hope, who purgest me from unclean affections, drawing mine eyes unto Thyself, and plucking my feet out of the snare.[1] I marvelled that other men should be alive, since he was dead whom I had loved as if he could never die, and I marvelled still more that I, his other self, should be alive when he was dead. Well did the poet say of his friend: "O thou half of my soul."[2] For I felt that my soul and his had been but one in

[1] Ps. xxv. 15.
[2] Horace, Odes, i. 3, 8. *Et serves animæ dimidium meæ*

two bodies; and life seemed horrible to me, because I was cut in two. And perhaps that is why I feared to die, lest the other half of him whom I had loved so dearly, should perish.

CHAPTER VII

How in the restlessness of sorrow he changed his abode.

O WHAT madness is this, which knows not how to love men, as men should love! O foolish man that I was, rebelling against the common lot of man! So I fumed, I sighed, I wept, I feared; I could find neither rest nor light. I carried about a torn and bleeding soul, which did not want to be carried; yet could I find no place to lay it down. In pleasant groves, amid sports or songs, or plats of flowers, in rich banquets, in the alcove or on the couch, in books and poetry, there was no peace. Everything, even the light of day, was gloom; all that was not my darling was wearisome and hateful, except sighs and tears. For in these alone I found some drops of comfort.

2. When my soul could not enjoy this solace, a load of misery crushed me down, which Thou alone, O Lord, couldst have lightened and removed. I knew it, but had neither will nor power, because I could not think of Thee as anything real or substantial. My deity was not

Thou, but an idle phantasm : my own error was my God. If I tried to lay down my burden in that vain abstraction, it slipped through the void and crushed me as before. I continued to be my own prison ; I could not live there, yet I could not escape. For whither could my heart flee from my heart ? whither could I flee from myself ? whither should I not pursue myself ? Yet I fled from my country, because my eyes would miss him less where they had not been accustomed to behold him. Thus from the town of Thagaste I came to Carthage.

CHAPTER VIII

How his grief was assuaged by time and the converse of friends.

TIME is not idle : nor is its flight unmarked ; through our senses it works wondrous changes in the mind. Lo, it came and went from day to day, and, as it came and went, it dropped into me other thoughts, other memories, gradually patching me up with the old familiar interests, which drove out my sorrow. Yet new sorrow, or at any rate the cause of new sorrow, took the place of the first. For how was it that my grief had pierced me so easily and so deeply, but that I had poured out my soul like water on the sand, by loving a mortal as if he would never die ? My greatest refreshment I found in the solace of new friends, who loved with me what I loved instead of Thee. And what I loved instead of Thee was a huge fable, a tedious lie, which tickled and seduced the foolish intelligence that lay itching in our ears.

2. But that fable did not die, when any of my friends died, because what charmed me in their intercourse was something altogether different. It was the talk, the laughter, the courteous mutual deference, the common study of the masters of eloquence, the comradeship now grave now gay, the differences that left no sting, as of a man differing with himself, the spice of disagreement which seasoned the monotony of consent. Each by turns would instruct or listen; the absent were always missed, the present always welcome. Such tokens springing from the hearts of mutual friends, and displayed by a word, a glance, an expression, by a thousand pretty complaisances, supply the heat which welds souls together, and make one of many.

CHAPTER IX

Of Human Friendship, and the blessedness of those who live in God.

THIS is what we prize in friendship; prize so highly that conscience stands self-accused, if it does not answer love with love, asking no personal gain beyond these proofs of goodwill.

Hence come the anguish of bereavement, the blackness of mourning, when joy is turned into bitterness, and the heart is steeped in tears, and the lost life of the dying is the death of the living. Blessed is he who loves Thee, and his friend in Thee, and his enemy for Thy sake. He alone loses no dear one, to whom all are dear in Him who is never lost. And who is this but our God, who made heaven and earth, and fills them all, because by filling He made them? Thee we never lose, unless we forsake; and, if we forsake, whither do we go, whither fly, but from Thy love to Thy wrath? For where do we fail to find Thy law in our punishment? And Thy law is Truth,[1] and Thou art Truth.[2]

CHAPTER X

Of the Transience of Created Things, wherein is no Rest.

TURN Thou us, O God of Hosts; shew us Thy countenance and we shall be saved.[3] For whithersoever the soul of man turns itself, it clings to sorrow, if not in Thee; yes, though it clings to what is fairest outside Thee and outside itself. Yet there would be nothing fair unless

---

[1] Ps. cxix. 42.　　　　　[2] John xiv. 6.
[3] Ps. lxxx. 19, agreeing with Ps. lxxix. 20 of the Vulgate.

I

from Thee came all that has birth and death.
By birth things begin to be, and grow towards
perfection; as soon as they are perfect, they wax
old and decay. Thus all wax old and all decay.
And when they are born and press towards Being,
the swifter their growth the swifter their flight
towards Not-Being. Such is their law.   So
much hast Thou appointed them, because they
are but parts, which may not all exist together,
but by their coming and their going make up the
whole whereof they are parts. Lo, even so is
our speech made up of vocal symbols; the
speech is not complete till each word has
uttered its part, and passes away to make room
for another.

2. From the midst of this fleeting show let my
soul praise Thee, O God, Creator of All, but let
not my senses have power to fasten her thereto
with the glue of desire. For the world, as it
goes its way towards not-being, rends her with
feverish longings; she wishes it to be, and yearns
to rest secure in what she loves. But in the
world is no place of rest, for it abides not; it
flies, and who can follow it with the eyes of
sense? Who can comprehend it, even when it is
close at hand? The eye of sense is slow, because
it is the eye of sense, and sense is its limit. It
can fulfil its proper task; but it cannot stop the
world, as it hurries on from its appointed beginning to its appointed end. For in Thy creative
Word all things hear their doom: "Hence and
thus far."

CHAPTER XI

*Of the unstability of Creation and the Changeless-
ness of God.*

BE not vain, O my soul, and suffer not the din
of thy vanity to deafen the ears of thy heart.
Do thou, too, listen. The Word Himself
calleth thee to return, and in Him is the un-
troubled place of rest, where love, that forsakes
not, is never forsaken. Behold, here one thing
goes and another comes, and this lowest whole is
formed by the succession of all its parts. " But
do I go away? " saith the Word of God.
There build thy home; there lay up the treasure
that thou hast thence received. Wearied at last
with vain deceits, O my soul, commit to the
Truth what the Truth gave thee; so shalt thou
lose nothing; thy withered flowers shall blossom
again, thy diseases shall be healed,[1] thy unstable
desires shall be re-shaped, renewed, braced up;
they shall not leave thee lying in that grave to
which they go down, but shall abide with thee
and stand fast in the presence of God, who
abideth and standeth fast for ever.[2]

2. Why wilt thou be perverse and follow after
thy flesh? Rather let the flesh turn and follow
thee. Whatsoever thou perceivest through the
flesh is a part, and thou knowest not the whole
of which it is a part; and yet the part delights

[1] Ps. ciii. 3.   [2] 1 Peter i. 23.

thee. But if thy fleshly sense could grasp the whole, if it were not, for thy punishment, justly restricted to a part of the whole, thou wouldest desire everything that here and now exists to vanish away, that so thou mightest love the All. For even what I say unto thee, thou hearest by the same fleshly sense, yet thou dost not wish the syllables to stand still, no, but to fly away, that others may come and thou mayest hear the whole.   It is the same with every unity that consists of a chain of parts.   If it can be felt as a whole, the chain is more beautiful than the links.   But more beautiful by far is our God, who made all things, who never goes away, because there is none to take His place.

CHAPTER XII

In all things pleasing God is to be loved.

IF bodies delight thee, praise God for them, and reflect thy love upon their Maker, lest, in what pleases thee, thou shouldest displease Him. If souls delight thee, let them be loved in God: for they too are changeful, and go their way, and perish, unless fixed and established in Him. Let them be loved, then, in Him. Whomsoever thou canst, bring swiftly to Him, and cry unto them, " Love Him, Love Him ; He made this world and is not far off. He did not make it and leave it, but all is from Him and in Him.

Lo, where the sweetness of truth is, there is He.
He dwells in the depth of the heart; but the
heart has gone astray from Him. Return, ye
transgressors, to your own heart,[1] and be rooted
in Him who made you. Stand with Him, and
ye shall stand. Rest in Him, and ye shall be
at rest. Why do ye flee into the desert, O why?
What you desire is good, for it is from Him; but
what is it in comparison with Him! Good it is,
and sweet it is; but justly will it become bitter,
because it is unjust to love the creature and forsake the Creator.

2. Why will ye still, still, tread these steep
and stony paths? Ye are seeking for rest, where
no rest is to be found. Seek what ye seek, but
it is not where ye seek it. Ye are seeking a
happy life in the land of death; it is not there.
For how can life be happy, where there is no
life at all? Our Life Himself came down to
earth, and bore our death, and slew it, by virtue
of the abundance of His life. With a voice of
thunder He cried to us to return to Him, into
that secret place whence He came forth, entering
first into the Virgin's womb, where He espoused
to Himself our created humanity, our mortal flesh,
that it might not be for ever mortal, and thence
proceeding like a bridegroom from his chamber,
and rejoicing as a giant to run His course.[2] He
tarried not but ran, crying aloud by His words,
by His deeds, by His death, by His life, by His
coming down, by His ascending again—crying

[1] Isa. xlvi. 8, agreeing with the Vulgate.
[2] Ps. xix. 5.

to us aloud to return to Him. And He departed
from our eyes, that we should return to our own
hearts, and find Him there.

3. For He departed, and lo, He is here. He
would not tarry long with us, yet did He never
leave us. For He went back to the heaven He
had never quitted, because the world was made
by Him, and He was in this world,[1] and came
into this world to save sinners.[2] To Him my
soul makes confession, that He may heal it, for
it hath sinned against Him.[3] O ye sons of men,
how long will ye be so slow of heart?[4] Life has
come down, and will ye not ascend and live?
Nay, ye have ascended, for ye are mounted on
high, and have set your face against heaven.[5]
Come down that ye may ascend, and ascend to
God.   For ye have but fallen by mounting
against Him.'' O my soul tell them this, that
they may weep in the valley of weeping,[6] and
thus bring them swiftly with thyself to God.
For thou tellest them these things by His Spirit,
if, while thou speakest, thou art burning with
the fire of love.

[1] John i. 10.
[2] 1 Tim. i. 15.   [3] Ps. xli. 4.
[4] Ps. iv. 3, agreeing with the Vulgate
[5] Ps. lxxiii. 9.
[6] Ps. lxxxiv. 6; compare Ps. lxxxiii. 6, 7 in the
Vulgate.

CHAPTER XIII

Of the cause of Love.

THIS was unknown to me at that time; hence
I loved beautiful things of the lower order,
and became more and more debased. I used to
say to my friends: "Do we love anything
except what is beautiful? What then is beautiful, and what is beauty? What is it that attracts
and attaches us to the things we love? For
unless they possessed some gracious form, they
would not touch us at all." And on consideration I perceived that in bodies there are
two things that deserve study; there is the
beauty of the composite, and again there is the
charm of perfect fitness and accommodation, as
for instance of the part to its whole, of the shoe
to the foot, and so forth. These ideas welled up
into my mind from the depths of my heart, and
so I came to write two or three books about the
Beautiful and the Fit. How many they were
exactly Thou knowest, O my God; I have
forgotten; I no longer possess them; they went
astray somehow or other.

CHAPTER XIV

*Of his books on the Beautiful and Fit which he
dedicated to Hierius.*

BUT what induced me, O Lord my God, to
address those books to Hierius, a professor of Rhetoric in Rome? I did not know

him even by sight, but I loved him for his high reputation, and I had been greatly struck by some passages from his speeches, which had been repeated to me. Yet the real reason was rather that others admired him, and could not praise him too warmly, because, being a Syrian by birth, trained at first in the Greek style, he had attained to high excellence in Latin oratory, and made himself a great name in philosophical studies also. Thus we praise and love those whom we have never seen. Does this love pass from the lips of the speaker to the heart of the listener? Impossible. One love kindles another. We love the man who is praised, because we believe that the praise comes from an honest heart, that is to say, from one who loves the man whom he praises. For that is how I loved men in those days, by the judgment of men, not by Thine, O my God, in whom none is deceived. But now the fame of Hierius was not like that of a notable charioteer or a popular matador; it was far more solid, and such as I should wish to gain myself. Now how was this?

2. For I should never have desired to be praised and loved as actors are, though I myself used to praise and love them. I would rather have been unknown, or even hated, than so loved or known. In what pigeonholes of the one soul are stored these different scales for weighing different inclinations? If I really hate a thing, and otherwise I should not shun and refuse it, how can I love it in another, when we are both men? You may love a good horse without wishing to

be one, even if it were possible; but the case of
an actor is different, for he shares our nature.
How can I love in a man, what I should hate to
be, seeing that I also am a man? What a
mystery is man himself, whose very hairs Thou
numberest,[1] O Lord, and they are never lost in
Thy sight; yet it is easier to count up the hairs
of his head, than his feelings and the movements
of his heart.

3. But my love for the famous orator was
such that I desired to be like him, and so I went
astray through pride, tossed about with every
wind[2] yet secretly piloted by Thee. Now how
do I know, how can I confess unto Thee with
certainty, that I loved Hierius rather in the love
of those who praised him, than for the gifts
for which they praised him? Because if those
very same people had blamed instead of praising,
and had told me just what they did in a tone of
blame and contempt, I should never have been
roused and kindled into affection for him. And
yet the gifts would have been the same, and
the man would have been the same, only the
feelings of the speaker would have been different.
How low lies this weak soul before she is rooted
in the rock of truth! With every puff of the
wind of opinion she veers and turns and twists
and twists again; her light is darkened and she
cannot see the truth, yet, lo, it is in full sight.
I thought it a great point gained, if I could bring
my style and my learning under the notice of
that famous man; though his praise would have

[1] Matt. x. 30.　　　　　[2] Eph. iv. 14.

been fuel to my fire, his censure would have wounded my empty and unguarded heart. Still I mused complacently on the Beautiful and the Fit, which had been the occasion of my addressing him, and admired the harmonious creations of my mind, though there was no one to share my pride of authorship.

CHAPTER XV

Why he could not understand the things of the spirit.

BUT as yet I could not see that this great question hinges upon Thy skill, O Almighty One, who alone makest wonderful things.[1] So my mind roamed among material forms ; the Beautiful I defined as that which is so in itself, the Fit as that which has a perfect relation to something else, and I gave material instances of both. I did indeed take into consideration the nature of mind, but my erroneous idea of spiritual existence prevented me from seeing the truth. The truth was actually forcing itself upon my eyes, but I turned away my affrighted reason from the incorporeal to outlines and colours and swelling bulks. I could not see these in my mind, and therefore I concluded that I could not see my mind. I loved the peace of virtue and hated the discord of vice ; in the former I discerned unity, in the latter a kind of division. The

[1] Ps. cxxxvi.

unity I conceived to be the rational intelligence, truth, and the chief good; in the division I saw a substantial irrational life, and the chief evil, which I held in my wretched folly to be not merely a substance but a kind of life, and yet not of Thee, O my God, of whom are all things. And yet I called the unity the *monad*, meaning by this a sexless intelligence, and the division the *dyad*, angry violence, that is, and vicious lust, not knowing what I was saying.

2. For I did not know, nor had I ever learned, that no substance is evil, and on the other hand, that even our intelligence is not the chief and unchangeable good. For as crimes arise when the capacity for anger is boastful, insolent and turbulent, and as vices come into action when the desire for carnal pleasures is unrestrained, so errors and false opinions stain life when the intelligence itself is corrupt, as it was then in me, not knowing that it must be irradiated by light from above, before it can participate in the truth, because it is not itself the essence of truth. For Thou shalt light my candle, O Lord my God, Thou shalt enlighten my darkness,[1] and of Thy fulness have we all received. For Thou art the true Light, that lighteth every man that cometh into this world.[2] For in Thee is no variableness neither shadow of turning.[3] But I was struggling towards Thee, yet was ever thrust back, that my wisdom might be death, for Thou resistest the proud.[4]

[1] Ps. xviii. 28.   [2] John i. 9, 16.
[3] James i. 17.   [4] 1 Peter v. 5.

3. For what pride, what madness was this, to maintain that I was by nature what Thou art! I knew that I was changeable, because the very reason why I sought for wisdom was that I might become better, and yet I chose rather to fancy that Thou wast changeable, than that I was not what Thou art. So I was thrust back; Thou didst resist my airy obstinacy, and I went on dreaming of material forms; flesh as I was, I scorned the flesh, wandering spirit that I was, I could not yet return to Thee.[1] Thus I wandered on after things that do not exist, either in Thee, or in me, or in the body. For they were not created by Thy truth, but devised by my own vanity from material existences. And so I used to ask Thy faithful little ones, my fellow-countrymen (to whom I was a foreigner though I knew it not)—I say I used to ask them in my foolish prating way: "Why then does the soul err if God created it?" But I did not like to be asked: "Why then does God err?" And I insisted that it was better to believe that Thy unchangeable substance was necessitated to err, than that my changeable substance had chosen to leave the right road, and was now erring as its punishment.

4. I was about twenty-six or seven when I wrote those volumes, deafened by material fancies, even while I was straining the ears of my heart to catch Thy secret melody, O sweet Truth. I was musing of the Beautiful and the Fit; I

[1] Ps. lxxviii. 39; but compare Ps. lxxvii. 39 of the Vulgate.

longed to stand and listen to Thee and rejoice greatly because of the Bridegroom's voice; [1] yet I could not, because I was charmed away by the call of my own error, and was sinking into the pit under the heavy load of my pride. For Thou didst not make me hear of joy and gladness, nor did my bones rejoice, for they were not yet humbled. [2]

CHAPTER XVI

How he understood books of the Liberal Arts without a Teacher.

AND what did it profit me that, when I was about twenty years old, I read by myself and understood the *Ten Categories* of Aristotle which had fallen into my hands. The title of that work had always sounded wonderful and divine, when my master, the Carthaginian rhetoric professor, and other learned men rolled it out, cracking their cheeks with pride. And now when I spoke about it with my fellows, they told me that they had hardly mastered it under learned teachers by dint of many lectures and diagrams drawn on sand, yet they could teach me nothing about it except what I had discovered in my own solitary reading. I saw clearly what it taught about substance, such as man, and all that belongs

[1] John iii. 29.
[2] Ps. li. 8, agreeing with Ps. l. 10 of the Vulgate.

to the substance, quality, that is to say, the man's figure; and quantity, how many feet high he is; and relation, whose brother he is; where he is placed; where he was born; whether he is standing or sitting, shod or armed, whether he is doing anything or suffering anything. I could understand all that falls under these nine classes, of which I have given some instances, or under the class of substance itself.

2. But what did all this profit me? Nay, it even hindered me, for, thinking that everything must be included in those ten predicaments, I endeavoured to find a place in them even for Thy mysterious and unchangeable Unity, O my God; as if Thou wast subject to Thy greatness and beauty, in the same way as a body is subject to its attributes. Thou art Thy greatness and Thy beauty, but a body is not great or beautiful because it is body, for, though it were smaller and less beautiful, it would be a body all the same. It was falsehood, not truth, that I thought about Thee, the forgery of my wretchedness, not the reality of Thy blessedness. For Thou hadst commanded that the earth should bring forth thorns and thistles for me, and that by the sweat of my face should I find bread,[1] and so it was done unto me.

3. And what did it profit me, the worthless slave of bad desires, that I read by myself and understood all the books of the so-called liberal arts that I could come by? I rejoiced in them, but I knew not whence came such truth and

[1] Gen. iii. 18, 19.

certainty as they had to offer. For my back
was turned to the light, and my face to the
reflection: hence the face, with which I saw the
reflection, was not touched by the light. Whatever books could teach me about rhetoric or
dialectic, or the dimensions of figures, or music,
or numbers, I learned with little difficulty and
no help (Thou knowest, O my God, that nimble
apprehension and acute discrimination are Thy
gift), but I did not make of these things a
sacrifice unto Thee. Thus they turned, not to
my profit, but to my destruction, because I was
eager to have so large a portion of my goods in
my own keeping, and left not my strength in
Thy keeping, but departed into a far-off land,
and wasted my substance on harlot desires. For
what profit could there be in a good thing put to
an evil use? For I did not perceive how hardly
these sciences are mastered even by the diligent
and clever, till I endeavoured to explain them
to my own pupils; and found that he was the
brightest scholar, who was not slower than the
rest in following my explanation.

4. But how could it all profit me, so long as
I thought that Thou, O Lord God, who art
Truth, wert an infinite luminous body, and that
I was a piece broken off that body. Strange
perversity! But so it was with me, nor am I
ashamed, O my God, to confess unto Thee
Thy mercy towards me, and to call upon Thee,
because then I was not ashamed to utter aloud
my blasphemies, and to bark against Thee.
What profited me then the nimbleness of my

intelligence in these doctrines, the knotty volumes that I unravelled with no help from human teacher, when in the doctrine of piety I was hideously, basely, sacrilegiously astray? Or how were Thy little ones hurt by their far slower understanding, since they forsook Thee not, but abode safe in the nest of Thy Church, where, nourished on wholesome beliefs, they fledged their pinions, and imped the wings of charity.

5. O Lord our God, under the shadow of Thy wings be our hope.[1] O protect and carry us. Thou wilt carry the little ones, yea, even to hoar hairs Thou wilt carry them.[2] For when Thou art our strength, our strength is strength indeed; when it is our own, it is but weakness. Our good ever lives in Thee; when we turn aside, we turn to evil. Turn us again now, O Lord, that we be not overturned. For Thou Thyself art our good; and therefore doth it live in Thee, and never faileth. Nor need we fear lest there be no home for us to return to. We fell from it; but our home, Thy eternity, has not fallen while we are away.

[1] Ps. lxiii. 8.   [2] Is. xlvi. 4.

BOOK V

HE describes the twenty-ninth year of
his age, in which he detected the
shallowness of Faustus, the Manichean, and abandoned his purpose of going on further in that
sect. In this year he was
appointed Rhetoric Professor at
Rome, and was thence sent to
discharge the same office at
Milan, where the sermons of
Ambrose opened his eyes, and
he determined to abjure Manicheeism and become once more
a Catechumen.

CHAPTER I

He calls upon his soul to praise God.

ACCEPT the sacrifice of my confessions from the hand of my tongue; Thou didst form it, and didst prompt it to confess unto Thy name. Heal all my bones, and let them say, " O Lord who is like unto Thee." [1] Not that he, who confesses unto Thee, makes known unto Thee what is passing within him : for the closed heart cannot bar Thy sight, nor can the hardness of man resist Thy hand. When Thou wilt Thou canst soften it, either by mercy or by chastisement ; and none can hide himself from Thy warmth. [2] But let my soul praise Thee, that it may love Thee ; and let it confess unto Thee all Thy mercies, that it may praise Thee. Thy whole creation praises Thee without ceasing, the spirit of man by his own lips which he turns towards Thee, things animate and inanimate by the lips of those who meditate upon them, to the end that, using Thy creatures as stepping stones, and passing on to Him who made them so wonderfully, our soul might shake off its despondence and soar up to Thee.   There is refreshment and true courage.

[1] Ps. xxxv. 10. [2] Ps. xix. 6.

CHAPTER II

*The wicked cannot escape the presence of God,
and therefore ought to turn to Him.*

LET the restless and unrighteous fly from
    Thee; yet Thou seest them, and Thine
eye pierceth the darkness. And, behold, they
live in a world of beauty, and they alone
are vile. And how have they hurt Thee,
or in what have they discredited Thy power,
whose just and sovereign rule extends from
heaven to the uttermost parts of creation?
Whither did they fly, when they fled from Thy
face? Where can they hide from Thee?
They fled, that they might not see Thee who
seest them; that they might be blinded and
run up against Thee. For Thou forsakest
nothing that Thou hast made.[1] The unjust
run up against Thee, that they may be justly
plagued, stealing away from Thy gentleness
and running up against Thy justice, and falling upon their own hardness. For in truth
they knew not that Thou art everywhere, and
that no place limits Thee, that Thou also art
present even with those who go far from
Thee.

2. O, that they might turn and seek Thee; for
though they have abandoned Thee, their creator,
Thou hast not abandoned Thy creatures. O, that

[1] Wisdom, xi. 25.

they might turn and seek Thee. And lo, Thou art there in their hearts, in the hearts of them that confess unto Thee, and cast themselves upon Thee, and weep in Thy bosom after all their weary wanderings. And Thy kind hand wipes away their tears, that they may weep the more and find joy in weeping. For Thou, Lord art not a man of flesh and blood. Thou art the Lord, who canst renew what Thou didst create, and canst console. Where was I myself when I was seeking Thee? Thou wast before me; but I had forsaken mine own self, and could not find myself—how much less then Thee?

CHAPTER III

Of Faustus the Manichean, and of the blindness of Philosophers who know the creature yet know not the Creator.

I WILL describe in the sight of my God the twenty-ninth year of my age. There was then at Carthage a Manichean bishop Faustus, a great snare of the devil, who entrapped many by the bait of his eloquence. This I admired; but I was beginning to distinguish the charm of words from the truth of things, which I was eager to learn, nor did I consider so much the beauty of the dish, as the kind of meat which their famous Faustus served up to me. For fame had run before him, as of one skilled in all honourable learning, and especially well versed in the liberal sciences.

2. And, since I was well read in the philosophers and had a good memory for their principles, I began to compare some of their doctrines with the tedious fables of the Manichees, and it struck me that probability was on the side of the philosophers, whose power reached so far that they were able to form a fair judgment of the world, although they did not find the Sovereign Lord of these His works.[1] For Thou art great, O Lord, and hast respect unto the lowly, but the proud Thou beholdest afar off.[2] Thou drawest near to none but the contrite in heart,[3] nor canst Thou be found by the proud, even though by inquisitive skill they number the stars and the sand, and map out the spaces of the constellations, and track the orbits of the heavenly bodies. For it is by mind and intelligence, which Thou bestowest, that they investigate these things. Much they have found out; they have foretold even beforehand the day, the hour, the extent of eclipses of those bright luminaries, the sun and moon : their calculations did not fail, and it came to pass as they foretold : they wrote down the rules they had discovered, so that to this day they may be read, and from them may be calculated in what year, in what month, on what day of the month, at what hour of the day, in what portion of its light, sun or moon will be eclipsed, and it will come to pass just as is predicted.

3. And men who know not, wonder and are

[1] Wisdom xiii. 9.   [2] Ps. cxxxviii. 6.   [3] Ps. xxxiv. 18.

amazed; and men who know are boastful and lifted up; in their ungodly pride they withdraw from Thy light into the shadow of eclipse; they can foresee the eclipse of the sun, and cannot see their own. For they do not ask, as religious men should, whence comes the intelligence whereby they investigate. And when they discover that Thou didst make them, they do not give themselves up to Thee, that Thou mayest preserve what Thou didst make, nor do they sacrifice unto Thee what they have made of themselves—slaying their high thoughts like fowls of the air, and their subtleties (wherein they dart along the secret paths of the deep) like fishes of the sea, and their lusts like beasts of the field— that Thou, O God, who art a consuming fire,[1] shouldest burn up their dead cares and renew them unto immortality.

4. But they know not the Way, Thy Word, by whom Thou didst create the things that are numbered, and the men who number them, and the senses by which they perceive what they number, and the intelligence whereby they number; nor do they know that of Thy Wisdom there is no number.[2] But Thy Only Begotten Himself was made unto us wisdom and righteousness and sanctification,[3] and was numbered amongst us, and paid tribute unto Cæsar.[4] They know not this Way, and deem that they are shining among the stars on high; and, lo, they have fallen to earth, and their foolish heart is darkened.[5]

[1] Deut. iv. 24.   [2] Ps. cxlvii. 5.   [3] 1 Cor. i. 30.
[4] Matt. xvii. 27.   [5] Rom. i. 21.

Much that is true do they teach about creation, but the Truth, the Artificer of creation, they do not piously seek, and therefore they find not. Or if they find, they know God, yet glorify Him not as God, neither are thankful, but become vain in their imaginations: they profess themselves to be wise,[1] claiming Thy attributes for their own, and hence, in the perversity of blindness, they ascribe to Thee those attributes that are their own, heaping lies upon Thee who art the Truth, changing the glory of the incorruptible God into an image made like to corruptible man, and to birds, and fourfooted beasts and creeping things, changing Thy truth into a lie, and worshipping and serving the creature more than the Creator.[2]

5. Yet I remembered many a true saying of the philosophers about creation, and I saw reason in their calculations, in the orderly sequence of times, and in the manifest attestation of the stars. This I compared with the doctrines of Manichaeus, who in his voluminous folly wrote many books on these matters. And here I could see no reason about the solstice, or the equinox, or eclipses, or whatever I had learned in books of secular philosophy. I was ordered to believe, but the ideas did not correspond with, nay, they contradicted, the rational theories established by mathematics, and indeed by the evidence of my own eyes.

[1] Rom. i. 21, 22.   [2] Rom. i. 23-25.

CHAPTER IV

Only the knowledge of God can make men happy.

IS a man pleasing to Thee, O Lord God of truth, because he knows these things? Nay, unhappy is the man who knows these, and not Thee; happy is the man who knows Thee, yet not these. And he who knows both Thee and these is not the more blessed for his learning; Thou alone art his blessing, if, knowing Thee as God, he glorifies Thee and gives Thee thanks, and becomes not vain in his imaginations.[1]

2. For as he who knows that he owns a tree, and gives thanks to thee for its use, although he knows not how many feet high it is, or how wide it spreads, is better than he who measures it and counts all its branches, yet neither owns it nor knows nor loves its Creator, so the faithful man, to whom belongs all the world of wealth, who having nothing yet possesseth all things[2] by his union with Thee, whom all things serve, though he know not even the circlings of the Great Bear, is better—it would be folly to doubt it—than he who measures the sky, and numbers the stars, and weighs the elements, and cares not for Thee, who hast ordered all things by measure and number and weight.[3]

N. 15

---

[1] Rom. i. 21.   [2] 2 Cor. vi. 10.
[3] Wisdom xi. 20.

CHAPTER V

The ignorance of Manichaeus about the stars makes him unworthy of trust in other things.

BUT yet who asked this Manichaeus to write about matters which do not help towards the learning of godliness? For Thou hast said to man, "Behold, godliness is wisdom,"[1] and of this he might have been ignorant, however perfectly he had known the other; nay, of this he must have been ignorant, or he would not so shamelessly have ventured to teach what he did not understand. For the ostentation of this worldly lore, even when it is sound, is nothing but vanity; godliness is confession unto Thee. From godliness he had gone astray, and all his show of learning only enabled the truly learned to perceive, from his ignorance of what they knew, how little he was to be trusted in abstruser matters. For he set no small value on himself, and endeavoured to persuade men that the Holy Ghost, the Comforter and Enricher of Thy faithful ones, dwelt in him personally with plenary authority.

2. And therefore, when he was detected in manifest errors about the sky, the stars, the movements of the sun and moon, although these are not articles of the faith, the impious presumption of the man became clearly manifest; for he taught

[1] Job xxviii. 28.

not merely what he did not know, but what was actually false, with pride so foolish and mad that he insisted on his own utterances as those of a divine person. For, when I hear an unlearned Christian brother talking wildly on matters of science, I can tolerate his idle opinions, and so long as he does not believe what is unworthy of Thee, O Lord, Thou Creator of all, I do not see that he is any the worse for not knowing how to apply the *Ten Categories* to the material creation. But he is the worse, if he thinks that such questions touch the essence of the creed, or ventures to assert dogmatically things of which he is ignorant.

2. And yet even this weakness is tolerated by our mother Charity in the infancy of faith, till the new man grows up into a perfect man, and is no longer blown about by every wind of doctrine.[1] But in the case of Faustus who, not content with being teacher, master, captain, chief of all whom he could persuade, dared to tell his people that in him they were following, not an ordinary man, but Thy Holy Ghost, surely, if he were once convicted of error, this mad arrogance should have been regarded with horror and utterly rejected. But I had not yet quite made up my mind whether the alternation of day and night, and of longer or shorter days and nights, and the eclipses of sun and moon, and whatever else of the same kind I had read about in other books, could be explained on his theory. If it could have been so explained, I should have doubted whether on

[1] Eph. iv. 13-14.

these points he was right or wrong, but I should have sacrificed my faith to his authority on account of his repute for sanctity.

CHAPTER VI

Faustus was eloquent but destitute of liberal education.

DURING almost the whole of the nine years that I listened with unsettled mind to the Manichean teaching, I was eagerly expecting the arrival of Faustus. For all members of the sect that I happened to meet, when they proved unable to solve my difficulties about natural science, used to refer me to him. He was coming, they said, and, if I would speak to him, all these problems—and greater ones too, if I liked to propose them—would be explained in the clearest way. When he came, I found him a man of charming manner and pleasant address, who said just what the others used to say, but in a much more agreeable style. The butler was most elegant, and the goblet was more costly, but my thirst remained. Already my ears had been satiated with such things ; and now they did not seem any better, because they were better said, nor true because dressed up in rhetoric, nor could I think the man's soul wise, because he looked wise and his speech was pleasing. Again, those who had engaged themselves for him were

not good judges; they thought him able and
wise, because his eloquence delighted them.

2. At the same time I perceived that there is
another kind of men, who regard even the truth
with suspicion, and will not accept it, if it is
delivered in polished and flowing language. But
me Thou hadst already instructed, O my God,
in ways wonderful and secret; and I believe
that it was Thou that didst teach me, because it
is the truth; for beside Thee there is no teacher
of truth, wherever and whencesoever it has shone
forth. Already I had learned from Thee, that
nothing ought to seem true because it is well
expressed, nor false because the word-symbols
are inelegant; yet again, that nothing is true
because rudely delivered, nor false because the
diction is brilliant; but that wisdom and folly
are like meats that are wholesome or unwhole-
some, and that either kind of meat can be served
up in silver or in delf, that is to say, in courtly
or in homely phrase. And so after eagerly
expecting Faustus all that time, I was delighted
with his gestures and ready sympathy, and with
the apt language that poured forth so easily to
clothe his ideas.

3. Yes, I was delighted, and like others, or
even beyond others, I praised and extolled him,
yet I was vexed that in the crowded lecture-
room I could not be allowed to impart my
difficulties to him in familiar converse, in the
give-and-take of discussion. As soon as I found
an opportunity for this, and gained his ear at a
time when questioning in the presence of my

friends was not unseemly, I laid before him some
of my doubts.   At once I discovered that he
possessed no tincture of the liberal arts excepting
grammar, and that, even of this, he had but the
ordinary knowledge.   He had read but a few
speeches of Tully, a very few treatises of Seneca,
a little poetry, and such books of his own sect
as were composed in good Latin ; this meagre
learning, eked out by the daily practice of speaking, was the sole foundation of his eloquence,
which owed its charm and seductiveness to
mother-wit and a certain natural grace.   Is it
as I remember, O Lord my God, Thou judge
of my conscience ?   Before Thee is my heart
and my memory, Who wast then guiding me by
the secret impulse of Thy providence, and wast
setting my shameful errors before my face,[1] that
I might see and hate them.

CHAPTER VII

How he was estranged from the Manichean sect.

FOR as soon as I clearly saw that Faustus was
    unskilled in the very sciences in which I
had thought him eminent, I renounced all hope
of his being able to open and resolve these perplexities that troubled me.   I perceived that
such ignorance need not indeed affect the sound-
ness of his religious faith, but only on condition

[1] Ps. l. 21.

of his not being a Manichee. The Manichean books are full of interminable fables about the sky and the stars, the sun and the moon, and greatly as I desired to discuss with him the mathematical arguments which I had learned elsewhere, and to ascertain whether the Manichean view was correct, or even tenable, I no longer expected that he would be able to explain things in a scientific way. But I must admit that, when I advanced my points for consideration and discussion, he behaved with modesty, and declined to undertake the task. He knew that he did not know, and was not ashamed to confess the fact. He was not one of the wordy crew from whom I had endured so much, who engaged to teach me all I wanted to know and said nothing. Faustus had a heart, which, if not right towards Thee, was honest towards himself. He was not absolutely ignorant of his ignorance, and he did not choose to be entangled by hasty assertions in a position where there was no way out or back; and for this I liked him all the better. For the modesty of candour is more beautiful than the problems which I desired to solve; and this I found to be his temper in all difficult and abstruse matters.

2. Hence the zeal with which I had plunged into the Manichean system was baffled. I despaired of the other doctors, when, as regards my own doubts, I had come to this judgment about their chief; and so I began to devote myself with Faustus to his favourite pursuit, the study of literature, in which I was already teach-

ing a class as rhetoric professor at Carthage. With him I read what he himself wished to read, or what I judged suitable to his character. But all my desire to make further progress in Manicheism fell dead as soon as I knew Faustus. I did not wholly separate from the Manichees, but out of vexation at finding nothing better, I made up my mind to be provisionally content with such conclusions as I had blundered upon, till something preferable should break upon my sight.

3. Thus the very Faustus, who had been to many a deadly snare, had begun, without willing or knowing it, to loose the snare in which I was caught. For Thy hand, O my God, in the mystery of Thy providence, did not betray my soul ; and my mother's heart-blood, poured forth in tears, was offered up for me day and night ; and Thou didst deal with me in wonderful secret ways. Thy doing was it, O my God, for the steps of a man are ordered by the Lord, and He shall choose his way.¹ Or what is the means of our salvation, but Thy hand recreating what Thou didst create ?

CHAPTER VIII

He sets out for Rome against the wish of his mother.

THOU didst so deal with me, then, that I was persuaded to go to Rome, and teach there what I was teaching at Carthage. Nor

¹ Ps. xxxvii. 23, agreeing with Ps. xxxvi. 23 of the Vulgate.

will I omit to confess unto Thee how I was persuaded, for, even in such things as this, we should notice and proclaim Thy secret workings and Thy ever-present compassion. I was not attracted to Rome by the richer fees or the higher dignity which my friends promised me (though these considerations affected my decision); but my chief and almost sole motive was that the students were said to be quieter there, and restrained by a severer discipline, so that they did not burst noisily into the class-rooms of other teachers, and indeed were not admitted at all without the permission of the lecturer.

2. On the other hand, at Carthage there is a disgraceful license of disorder among the students. They burst shamelessly into the room, and with the demeanour of madmen break up the discipline which the teacher has established for the better progress of his pupils. Many things they will do with the utmost effrontery which are real outrages punishable by law, if it were not that custom has sanctioned them; a custom which proves them the more unhappy, because it allows them to do what Thy eternal law never will allow. And they think that they act thus with impunity, though the very blindness with which they act is their punishment; and they suffer infinitely more harm than they inflict. So it came to pass that, as a teacher, I was compelled to endure in others the evil habits which, as a student, I had refused to adopt; and on this account I was glad to remove to a place where, as I was assured by men who knew, such con-

duct was not tolerated. But in truth Thou, my Hope and Portion in the land of the living,[1] in order that I might change my earthly abode for the salvation of my soul, wast driving me forth from Carthage and alluring me to Rome, by the agency of men who loved this death-in-life—by their mad doings in the one place and their empty promises in the other—and to correct my wanderings wast secretly making use both of their perversity and of mine. For those who disturbed my leisure with their horrid frenzy were blind, and those who invited me elsewhere thought but of earth. For myself, I loathed a real misery in the one place, and craved for a false happiness in the other.

3. But why I departed hence and went thither Thou knewest, O my God; but Thou shewedst it neither to me nor to my mother, who grieved deeply over my departure, and followed me down to the shore. She clasped me tight in her embrace, willing either to keep me back or to go with me: but I deceived her, and pretended that I had a friend whom I could not leave, till the ship set sail. Thus I lied to my mother, and such a mother! And I escaped; for this, too, Thou didst mercifully forgive, and preserve me, fool that I was, from the waters of the sea unto the water of Thy grace, that, when I was washed therein, Thou mightest dry the streams of my mother's tears, with which she daily watered the ground beneath her face as she prayed to Thee for me. Yet she refused to go home without

[1] Ps. cxlii. 3.

me, and I hardly persuaded her to pass the night in a memorial chapel of the blessed Cyprian hard by the ship. But in that night I secretly set forth, and she remained to pray and weep. And what was she beseeching of Thee, O my God, with all those tears, but that Thou wouldest prevent me from sailing? But Thou, in Thy hidden wisdom, didst grant the substance of her desire, yet refuse the thing she prayed for, in order that Thou mightst effect in me what she was ever praying for.

4. The wind blew and filled our sails, and the shore receded from our gaze. There was she in the morning, wild with sorrow, besieging Thine ears with complaints and sighs which Thou didst not regard, for by my desires Thou wast drawing me to the place where I should bury my desires, and her carnal yearning was being chastened by the appointed scourge of grief. For she loved to keep me with her, as mothers are wont, yes, far more than most mothers, and she knew not what joy Thou wast preparing for her out of my desertion. She knew not: therefore she wept and cried, and by that anguish revealed the taint of Eve, seeking with groans what with groans she had brought forth. Yet when she had made an end of accusing my deceit and my cruelty, she fell again to praying for me, and so returned to her house, while I went on my way to Rome.

CHAPTER IX

How he nearly died of a fever.

AND, behold, there I fell under the rod of
bodily sickness, and was going down
unto hell carrying with me the many grievous
misdeeds that I had committed against Thee
and myself and others, in addition to the chain
of original sin, whereby we all die in Adam.[1]
For Thou hadst not forgiven me anything in
Christ, nor had He atoned in His Flesh the
enmity[2] against Thee into which I had come
by my sins.   For how could He atone it in
that phantasmal flesh which I attributed to Him ?
The death of my soul, therefore, was as real as
the death of His Flesh seemed imaginary, and
the life of my soul was as imaginary as the
death of His Flesh (which I did not believe)
was real.   And now my fever grew worse, and I
was panting and perishing.   For whither should
I have gone, if I had then departed, but into
fire and torments such as my deeds deserved
in the justice of Thy ordinance ?   And my
mother knew not this, yet was she praying for
me far away.   But Thou, who art everywhere
present, didst hear her where she was, and
hadst pity on me where I was, so that I recovered the health of my body, though still
mad with impiety of heart.   For *in* all that

[1] 1 Cor. xv. 22.   [2] Eph. ii. 14.

grave peril I never wished for Thy baptism; I was better when, as a boy, I begged it of my mother's piety, as I have already recollected and confessed.

2. But my shame had grown with me, and I laughed like a fool at Thy healing art, Who didst not suffer me, evil as I was, to die the second death. Had my mother's heart been smitten with that wound, it never could have been healed. For I cannot express her tender love towards me, or with how far greater anguish she travailed of me now in the spirit, than when she bore me in the flesh. And so I do not see how she could have been healed, if such a death of mine had pierced through the bowels of her love. And where would have been her prayers, so fervent and so incessant? Nowhere, but in Thy keeping. But couldest Thou, O God of pity, despise the humble and contrite heart [1] of that chaste and ascetic widow, so constant in almsgiving, so reverent and serviceable to her saints, who never for one day omitted to bring her oblation to Thy altar. Twice in the day, at morning and evening, she went without fail to Thy church, not for empty fables or old wives' gossip, but that she might hear Thee in Thy instructions, and that Thou mightest hear her in her prayers.

3. Couldest Thou despise the tears with which she begged of Thee, not gold or silver nor any perishable fleeting good, but the salvation of her son's soul? Couldest Thou, by

[1] Ps. li. 17.

whose grace she was what she was, refuse to help her? Surely not, O Lord. Nay, Thou wast present, and wast listening, and bringing all to pass in the manner Thou hadst predestined. Impossible that Thou couldest deceive her in those visions and prophetic utterances (some I have recorded, some I have not), which she stored in her faithful heart, and pressed upon Thee in constant prayer as Thy own handwriting. For, since Thy mercy endureth for ever,[1] to those whom Thou forgivest all their debts Thou dost condescend to make Thyself debtor by Thy promises.

CHAPTER X.

Of his errors before he came to believe in the Gospel.

THOU didst heal my sickness then, and to save the son of Thy handmaid, for the time in respect of his body, that he might live to receive from Thee a better and more abiding health. And even then I joined myself to those deceived and deceiving " saints," not merely to their " hearers" (of whom the friend, in whose house I had fallen sick and recovered, was one), but to those whom they call "elect." For as yet I held that it is not we who sin, but that some alien nature sins in us; and my pride de-

[1] Ps. cxviii.

lighted in the thought that I was not to blame, and that, when I had done evil I need not confess that I had done it, to the end that Thou mightest heal my soul, because I had sinned against Thee.[1] But I loved to excuse my soul, and lay the guilt on something else, which was with me and was not myself. But in truth I was one, and nothing but my iniquity had divided me against myself; and the thought that I was not a sinner was the deadlier part of my sin; and my abominable wickedness was that I preferred that Thou, O Almighty God, that Thou shouldest be overcome in me to my own destruction, than that I should be overcome by Thee to my own salvation. Not yet, then, hadst Thou set a watch before my mouth and a door of self-control about my lips, that my heart should not turn aside to froward words, to make vain excuses for my sins with men that worked iniquity.[2] Therefore I still combined with their "elect," though I already despaired of making any real progress in my false doctrine, and I even began to hold slackly and carelessly the very tenets with which I had determined to satisfy myself, if I could find nothing better. For the thought sprang up in my mind that the wisest philosophers were the Academics, who held that all is doubtful, and that certainty is unattainable by man. For this I thought, as most people do, was their obvious meaning; as yet I did not catch their drift either.

3. Nor did I forbear openly to check my host

[1] Ps. xli. 4.   [2] Ps. cxli. 3-4.

in the implicit trust which I perceived him to repose in the fables wherewith the Manichaean books are stuffed full. Yet I lived in greater familiarity with them than with others, who were not embarked in that heresy. I did not defend it with the same keenness as of old; yet the friendship of these men (and there were many lurking in Rome) disinclined me to look for anything else, the more so because I despaired of finding truth in Thy church, O Lord of heaven and earth, Creator of all things visible and invisible; for from this they had alienated me. It seemed to me utterly shameful to believe that God could wear the form of human flesh, and be limited by the material outline of such a frame as ours. When I wished to think of my God, I could think of nothing but corporeal substance (for I did not believe that anything else exists at all), and this was the chief and almost the sole cause that made my errors inevitable.

4. For, because of this, I held that there was a corporeal substance of evil also, having its own ugly and misshapen bulk,—whether it were coarse (in which case they called it earth) or fine and subtle, like the substance of the air, which they conceive of as a malignant intelligence permeating that earth. And because piety, in any case, forced me to believe that God is good, and cannot have created an evil nature, I held that there were two antagonistic material substances, both infinite, yet so that the evil was less and the good greater. From this pestilent beginning all my other blasphemies came upon me. For when

my mind endeavoured to turn back to the Catholic faith I was repelled, because the Catholic faith was not what I thought it was. I judged it more religious to suppose that Thou, O my God, to whom Thy mercy makes confession by lips, wert infinite on all sides but one (for where evil was opposed I was compelled to acknowledge Thee finite), than that Thou wert wholly limited by the form of a human body.

5. And I thought it better to believe that Thou hadst created no evil—because in my ignorance I held that evil was not only a substance but a material substance, and this again because I could form no conception of mind except as a fine substance diffused through space—than to admit that such a substance, as I held evil to be, could have come from Thee. Even our Saviour, Thy Only begotten, I imagined to have been shot forth for our salvation from the bright mass of Thy bulk in such a way that I could not hold any belief about Him, except what I could imagine in my vanity. If His nature were such it could not, I thought, have been born of the Virgin Mary without being blended with the flesh. And I did not see how it could be blended without being defiled, if it were such as I figured it to myself. Hence I feared to believe that he was born in the flesh, lest I should be compelled to believe that He was defiled by the Flesh. Now will Thy spiritual ones gently and lovingly laugh at me, if they read these *Confessions*; yet this is what I was.

CHAPTER XI

Of his relations with the Catholics.

AGAIN I thought it not possible to answer the objections of the Manichees to Thy Scriptures; yet at times I felt a wish to discuss them, point by point, with some one really learned in the Scriptures, and to find out what he thought about them. For before this the discourses of one Helpidius, who used to speak and dispute openly against these same Manichees, had made an impression on me while I was at Carthage; for he brought forth arguments from Scripture which could not easily be rebutted, and I thought that their answer was weak.

2. They were shy of producing it in public; but, when they were speaking esoterically, they used to tell us that the books of the New Testament had been falsified by some one or other, who wished to engraft the Jewish law upon the Christian faith. Yet they never produced any unadulterated copies. But chiefly I was bound and choked and crushed down into materialism by those "bulks;" under this load I groaned, and could not breathe the clear pure air of Thy Truth.

CHAPTER XII

How Students at Rome defrauded their Teachers.

I BEGAN diligently to apply myself to the object that had brought me to Rome, the teaching of the art of rhetoric. And first I gathered at my house a little company of scholars, to whom and by whom I was beginning to be known; when, lo, I discovered that there were vexations at Rome from which I had been free in Africa. It was true, as appeared, that young profligates did not practise "wreckings" here, but "all of a sudden," said my friends, "a number of them will enter into a plot to escape paying their fees, and march off to another teacher," breaking their faith and despising justice for love of money. These also my heart hated, though not with a perfect hatred.[1] For perhaps I hated them more because I was likely to suffer from them, than because they were ready to treat anybody in the same lawless fashion.

2. Yet certainly those who do such things are base and play the harlot away from Thee, loving the fleeting delusions of time and filthy lucre which pollutes the hand that grasps it; clasping the world that flies, despising Thee who abidest and recallest and forgivest the adulterous soul that returns to Thee. Even now I hate such base and crooked people, though I love to reform them, and teach them to prize learning above money, and Thee, O God—Who art truth and plenteousness of unfailing good and peace unstained—above learning itself. But at that time I had more dislike of their badness for my own sake, than desire of their amendment for Thine.

[1] Ps. cxxxix. 22.

CHAPTER XIII

He is sent to teach Rhetoric at Milan and is there received by Ambrose.

AND so, when the Milanese sent to Rome, requesting the prefect of the city to provide them with a teacher of rhetoric, and to furnish him for the journey at the public expense, I made application, through those very Manichaean fanatics, from whom my going was to detach me, though neither they nor I foresaw this result, to Symmachus, who was the prefect, desiring him that upon due examination I might have the post. So I came to Milan, where I found the Bishop Ambrose, Thy godly servant, known throughout the world as one of the best of men, whose eloquent discourses were at that time diligently supplying to Thy people the fatness of Thy wheat, the gladness of Thy oil, and the sober intoxication of Thy wine.[1] By Thee was I led blindly to him, that by him I might be led with open eyes to Thee. That man of God received me as a father, and welcomed the stranger like a true bishop.

2. And I began to love him, not at first as a teacher of the truth, which I despaired of finding in Thy church, but as a fellow-creature who was kind to me. I listened attentively to his sermons, not with the right attitude of mind, but

[1] Ps. iv. 7; civ. 15.

criticising his eloquence, whether it was equal to
his reputation, whether its stream was broader
or narrower than men reported. Thus I hung
eagerly upon his expressions, while as regards
his subject I remained a cool or contemptuous
looker-on, delighted only with the charm of his
style, which though more learned was not so
exhilarating or soothing as that of Faustus. But
as regards their subject matter there was no comparison; for the one was wandering in Manichaean
fallacies, the other was teaching the way of life
in all sincerity. But salvation is far from sinners[1]
such as I was then; yet was I gradually drawing
towards it, though I knew not.

CHAPTER XIV

*He is gradually enlightened by the teaching of
Ambrose.*

FOR though I cared not to understand what
he said, but only to hear how he said it
(for since I had begun to despair that there was
any road whereby man might approach Thee this
idle taste alone was left), yet, with the phrases
which I loved, the facts which I neglected began
to trickle into my mind, because I could not keep
them apart. And, while I opened my heart to
welcome the eloquence of his speech, I began,
though only step by step, to feel also the truth of

[1] Ps. cxix. 155.

his speech. For first of all I began to perceive that what he said could be defended; I no longer thought that the Catholic faith, for which I had fancied that no sort of case could be made out against the Manichæan objections, could not be maintained with self-respect; especially after I had heard one difficulty after another in the ancient Scriptures explained by way of allegory. For while I read those Scriptures in the letter, I was slain in the spirit.[1]

2. And so, when many passages in the Bible had been explained, I began to blame my own despair for believing that no resistance at all could be made to those who hated and ridiculed the Law and the Prophets. Yet I did not think that I ought to hold the Catholic way, because it also happened to have learned champions, who could meet objections with abundant and by no means contemptible rejoinders; nor did I consider it a sufficient reason for condemning my own opinions if both sides appeared to be defensible. I judged Catholicism not vanquished yet not victorious. At this point I began earnestly to consider whether there were any conclusive proof by which I could refute the errors of Manicheeism. Had I been able to conceive of a spiritual substance, all their devices would have been broken, and I could have shaken them off; but this as yet I found impossible.

3. However, the more I considered and compared the more I saw that most of the philosophers had held a far more probable opinion about

[1] 2 Cor. iii. 6.

the frame of the world and all that nature which the bodily senses perceive. And so though in academic fashion, or what is commonly thought such, I doubted at everything and wavered to and fro, yet I made up my mind to abandon the Manichæans, considering it wrong in the very midst of my doubts to adhere to a sect which I judged inferior to more than one school of philosophy. Yet I absolutely refused to commit the healing of the sickness of my soul to these philosophers, because they knew not the saving Name of Christ. I resolved, therefore, to be a catechumen in the Catholic Church, which had been commended to me by my parents, till some sure light should arise to direct my path.

BOOK VI

Of the arrival of Monnica at Milan,
and how, in his thirtieth year,
Augustine was brought by the
sermons of Ambrose to a clearer
understanding of the Catholic
truth, which the Manichaeans
perversely attacked. He describes the character of his friend
Alypius, and his acquaintance
with Nebridius. He tells of the
mental anguish into which he
was thrown by the thought of a
new and better life, and how the
fear of death and judgment drove
him daily nearer to conversion.

M

CHAPTER I

Augustine is neither Manichee nor Catholic.

O THOU, who hast been my hope from my
youth upwards, where wast Thou, and
whither hadst Thou gone from me? Didst not
Thou create me, and make me to differ from the
four-footed beasts and the fowls of the air?
Thou didst make me wiser; yet was I wandering along a dark and slippery road; I was seeking Thee outside of myself, and could not find
the God of my heart; I had come into deep
waters, and doubted and despaired of finding
truth. By this time my mother had come to
me, brave in her piety, following me over land
and sea, fearless in all perils through faith in
Thee. For in the height of the storm she
encouraged even the sailors, whose office it is to
soothe the alarms of voyagers unacquainted with
the deep, promising them that they should come
safe to land, because Thou hadst promised her
this in a vision.

2. She found me in sore peril, through
despair of discovering the truth. But when I
had told her that I was no longer a Manichee,
though not yet a Catholic Christian, she was not

filled with delight at this unexpected good news,
relieved though she was of that half of her
misery, which caused her to weep over me as one
dead yet not past recall, and to carry me forth, as
it were, upon a bier that Thou mightest say to
the son of the widow, "Young man, I say unto
thee, arise," and that so he should arise and
begin to speak, and Thou mightest restore him
to his mother.[1]   I say her heart was not uplifted
with a tumult of joy, when she heard that what
she daily besought with tears was already in great
part obtained, that, though I had not yet grasped
the truth, I had still been rescued from error.
No, but because she was confident that Thou,
who hadst promised all, wouldest grant what yet
was lacking, she answered calmly with a bosom
full of trust, "She believed in Christ, that before
she departed this life she should see me a faithful
Catholic."

3. This she said to me.   But to Thee, O
Fount of Pity, faster than ever did she pour forth
tears and prayers, that Thou wouldest make haste
to help and lighten my darkness.   More zealously
than ever did she speed to church, there to hang
upon the lips of Ambrose, as a fountain of water
springing up to eternal life.[2]   She loved that
great man as an angel of God,[3] because she had
learned that by his instrumentality I had been
brought for a while to a state of wavering.
Through this she felt assured that I should

---

[1] Luke vii. 14, 15.   [2] John iv. 14.
[3] Gal. iv. 14

recover my health, though not without surmounting still graver danger, as my fever grew to its height, or what physicians call the crisis.

CHAPTER II

Of Feasts and Meetings at the Tombs of the Martyrs.

AND so when she came to the memorials of the saints, and was forbidden by the doorkeeper to carry in the cakes, bread and wine, which she had brought with her according to African use, as soon as she learned that it was against the bishop's orders, she submitted, so piously and dutifully that I myself wondered to see how willingly she renounced her own practice, rather than dispute his commands. For her spirit was not deafened by sottish cravings, nor did the love of wine provoke her to hate the truth, as is the case of too many, both men and women, whose gorge rises at the hymn of temperance as at a cup of water. But she, though she brought a basket full of the usual viands, to be tasted by herself and then given away, never set on the table more than one little cup of wine, diluted to suit her own abstemious taste, in order that she might satisfy the requirements of her position. And, if she was called upon to attend many such memorials of the dead, she carried the same little cup wherever she went, permitting her friends to take only the merest sip, so that the contents became little better than lukewarm water; because in this she sought not pleasure but devotion.

2. And so, when she learned that that illustrious preacher and godly prelate had forbidden these things to be done, even by those who did them in all sobriety, lest any occasion of excess should be given to the intemperate, and further because these memorials were too like the superstitious *Parentalia* of the Gentiles, she willingly submitted, and in place of her basket full of fruits of the earth, she learned to bring to the Memorials of the Martyrs a bosom full of purer offerings, so that she might give what she could to the poor, and the communion of the Lord's Body, in imitation of whose Passion the martyrs were sacrificed and crowned, might be celebrated at the Memorials in this way.

3. And yet it seems to me, O Lord my God, and this is the thought of my heart in Thy sight, that perchance my mother would not so readily have agreed to the abolition of this usage, if it had been ordained by one whom she loved less than Ambrose, whom she loved deeply for my salvation. And he loved her for her godly conversation which led her so constantly to church, fervent in spirit and in all good works, so that often, when he saw me, he broke out into her praises, congratulating me because I had such a mother. Little he knew what a son she had in me, who doubted about everything, and deemed that the way of life could not possibly be found.

CHAPTER III

The Labours and Studies of Ambrose.

NOR did I groan in prayer for Thy help, but my mind was intent to seek and eager for dispute. Ambrose himself I counted one of the happy ones of this world, because he was held in such honour by the great; only I thought that celibacy must be a burden upon him. But what hopes he cherished, what battles he had to fight against the temptation of that very eminence, what solace he found in adversity, what sweet joys he tasted in Thy bread with the spiritual mouth of his heart—all this I could not so much as guess, because I had no experience. Nor did he know my fever, nor the deep pit of my jeopardy. For I could not ask him what I wanted as I wanted, because the shoals of busy people, to whose infirmities he ministered, came between me and his ear and lips. And in the few moments when he was not thus surrounded, he was refreshing either his body with needful food or his mind with reading. While he read his eye wandered along the page and his heart searched out the meaning, but his voice and his tongue were at rest.

2. Often when we attended (for the door was open to all, and no one was announced), we saw him reading silently, but never otherwise, and after sitting for some time without speaking (for

who would presume to trouble one so occupied?)
we went away again.   We divined that, for the
little space of time which was all that he could
secure for the refreshment of his mind, he allowed
himself a holiday from the distraction of other
people's business, and did not wish to be interrupted; and perhaps he was afraid lest eager
listeners should invite him to explain the harder
passages of his author, or to enter upon the discussion of difficult topics, a task which would run away
with his leisure and hinder him from perusing as
many volumes as he wished.   Yet it may be that
the reason for his silent reading was the necessity
for sparing his voice, which was very easily
injured.   In any case the reason that guided such
a man must have been good.

3. But so it was that I found no opportunity
of consulting the holy oracle of his breast, except
in brief audiences.   The flood of my difficulties
could only be poured out to a listener with
abundant leisure at his disposal, and such an one
I could not find.   Yet I heard Ambrose rightly
handling the word of truth [1] before the people
every Lord's day, and I became more and more
certain that it was possible to unravel all the webs
of wily sophistry woven by our deceivers against
the divine books.

4. But when I learned that the words "man
was made in Thy image," [2] were not understood
by Thy spiritual sons, whom by Grace Thou
hast regenerated of the Catholic Mother, as
signifying that Thou art limited by the form of a

[1] 2 Tim. ii. 15.   [2] Gen. i. 27.

human body, although I could form no idea, not even by way of allegory, of the true nature of spiritual substance, yet I was both glad and ashamed to find that for all these years I had been barking, not against the Catholic faith, but against the vain devices of carnal thoughts. Certainly I had been rash and impious in this, that, what I ought to have said in the tone of an enquirer, I had said in that of an accuser. For Thou, who art highest and nearest, most distant yet most present, who hast not parts greater and parts less, but art wholly everywhere and yet nowhere, assuredly art not of bodily shape, yet didst Thou make man in Thy image, and, lo, from head to foot he is in space.

CHAPTER IV

He begins to understand the Doctrine of the Church from the Sermons of Ambrose.

SINCE then I did not know in what manner this Thy image subsisted, I ought to have knocked and enquired how it was to be believed, not scornfully to have resisted what I thought was believed. And therefore the gnawing perplexity what I could still hold as certain, was sharpened by shame that, mocked and deceived by the promise of certainty, I had for so long a time, with childish blunders and petulance, babbled of uncertainties as if they were certain.

For that they were altogether false did not become clear to me till later. Only I was certain that they were uncertain, and that I had for a time regarded them as certain, while I was blindly accusing Thy Catholic Church, which did not teach what I so severely denounced; though I had not yet discovered that what she did teach was the truth. So I was confounded; I was on the way to conversion and I rejoiced, O my God, to learn that Thy One Church, the Body of Thy One Son, in which the Name of Christ had been put upon me as an infant, did not believe childish absurdities, did not in her sound doctrine teach that Thou, the Creator of all, wast imprisoned in space, eminent indeed and vast, yet bounded by the figure of human limbs.

2. I rejoiced, also, because I was enabled to read with other eyes those ancient Scriptures of the Law and the Prophets, which used to seem so absurd, while I was reproving Thy saints for thi king what they never thought. Gladly did I hear Ambrose, in his sermons to the people, insisting upon the words, "the letter killeth but the spirit giveth life,"[1] as a rule most carefully to be observed; taking off the mystic veil and opening the spiritual sense of those passages which in their literal acceptation seemed to teach folly; never saying anything that could offend me, though

---

[1] 2 Cor. iii. 6. When Augustine says that he would not "climb" he is thinking of the allegoric mode of interpretation, which was called the *Anagoge* or "way up." In the word "halter," *suspendio*, there is an allusion to the Academic "suspense."

I could not tell as yet whether what he said was true. For I would not allow my heart to climb, avoiding the precipice to die by the halter. For I wanted to be as certain of things unseen as I was that seven and three make ten.

3. For I was not so crazy as to think that not even this could be known, but I wanted to have the same assurance of all other things as of this, whether of things corporeal which were not immediately present to my senses, or things spiritual about which I could form none but a corporeal idea. I might have been healed by belief, directing my purified sight in some way towards Thy truth, which ever abides and never fails in any part. But as one who has suffered under a bad physician is afraid to trust himself even to a good one, so was it with the health of my soul, which certainly could only be cured by belief, yet refused to be cured, lest it should believe what was false, resisting Thy hands, who hast compounded the prescriptions of faith, and applied them to all the diseases of the world, and stamped them with an authority so high.

CHAPTER V

Of the Authority and Necessity of Holy Writ.

BUT from this time I began even to prefer the Catholic doctrine, perceiving that the church, which enjoined men to believe what was not proved (it might be provable, though not

to everybody, or it might not be provable at
all), was more modest and more candid than
the Manichees, who gibed at credulity, made
rash promises of scientific knowledge, and then
went on to commend belief in the most fabulous
nonsense, because it could not be proved. Then
gradually Thou, O Lord, stroking and soothing
my heart with gentle and most merciful touch,
didst bring me to consider what hosts of things I
believed though I had never seen nor witnessed
them, about the history of mankind, about places
and cities which I had never visited, about
friends, about physicians, about all kinds of men
—things which we must believe, if we are to do
anything at all—lastly, how absolutely fixed was
my faith as to the parents from whom I was
born, though I could only know this by believing
what I had heard. And thus Thou didst con-
vince me that the blame lay not upon those who
believed Thy books, which Thou hast established
with authority so high among almost all nations,
but upon those who did not believe them, and
that I ought not to listen to those who might
ask: "How do you know that these books were
given to mankind by the Spirit of the One true
and most truthful God?" For that was the
very thing that was most credible, since not all
the vehement quibbling that I had read in the
volumes of so many mutually destructive philosophers could force me even for a moment to doubt
that Thou art, though I knew not what Thou
art, or that the government of human life belongs
to Thee.

2. I believed this sometimes more firmly, sometimes more feebly; yet this I did always believe that Thou art, and Thou hast a care for us, although I knew not what to think about Thy Nature, or what road leads, or leads back, to Thee. And so, since we are too weak to discover the truth by the mere light of reason, and for this cause need the authority of Holy Writ, I began to believe that Thou never wouldest have assigned such eminent and world-wide authority to Scripture, unless it had been Thy will that through it Thou shouldest be believed, and through it sought. For by this time I could find an explanation for the contradictions that used to repel me in the depth of its mysteries, having heard many of them reasonably explained, and its authority appeared to me all the more august, and all the more worthy of reverential faith, because, while all might read it, it shrouded the grandeur of its inmost thought within the deeper meaning, appealing to all by its plain and homely speech, and tasking the attention of those who are not light of heart, welcoming all in its hospitable arms, and guiding to Thee through narrow crannies a few, yet far more than it could have done, if its authority were not so highly exalted that it drew the multitude within the bosom of its holy humility. On these things did I muse, and Thou wast with me; I sighed and Thou didst hear; I tossed upon the waves, and Thou didst steer; I travelled along the world's broad highway, and Thou didst not forsake me.

CHAPTER VI

*Of the misery of Ambition and the example of a
jolly Beggar.*

MY heart was set upon promotion, gain, the
married life ; and Thou wast laughing me
to scorn.   In those lusts did I endure the
bitterest vexations ; Thou wast proving Thy
favour by marring the sweetness of all that was
not Thyself. Behold my heart, O Lord, who
hast willed that I should remember this, and
confess it unto Thee. For Thou didst free my
soul from the clinging deadly birdlime, and now
it cleaves unto Thee. How unhappy was it !
and Thou didst quicken the smart of its wound
that it should leave all else and turn to Thee,
who art above all, without whom nothing could
exist, that it should turn and be healed. How
unhappy was I, and how didst Thou make me
feel my unhappiness on that well-remembered
day ! I was preparing a panegyric to be delivered
in presence of the Emperor, in which I was to
utter many an untruth, and to be applauded by
those who well knew that they were untruths ;
my heart was panting under this burden, and
throbbing with the fever of morbid thoughts, when,
as I walked through one of the streets of Milan,
I observed a poor beggar ; I suppose he had had
a good meal, and he was joking and laughing.
At this I sighed, and spoke to my companions of

the many sorrows that attend our insane pursuits, how that all our labours, such as that which I was then engaged in, tugging at the load of my misery beneath the goad of lust and making it heavier by tugging, had no other aim than the attainment of peaceful enjoyment, which that beggar had found before us, and we perhaps should never find at all. For what he had already secured at the cost of a few pence tossed to him in alms, the joy, that is to say, of temporal felicity, I was still pursuing through long and weary byways.

2. His indeed was not the true joy, yet far less true was that which I was seeking by my ambitious schemes. And certainly he was glad, while I was anxious; he was at peace, and I was full of alarm. If anyone had asked me whether I would rather be merry or fearful, I should have answered "merry." Again if he had asked me whether I would rather be that beggar or myself, I should have answered "myself," wearied as I was with cares and fears; but only out of perversity, for could it be so in truth? For I could not count myself happier because I was more learned; my learning gave me no pleasure; I was only using it to flatter men—not to teach them but only to flatter. Wherefore also Thou was breaking my bones with the staff of Thy discipline.

3. Away from my soul then those who say unto her: "There is a difference in the source of joy; that beggar's joy lay in tippling, you were seeking the joy of glory." Glory, O my Lord, which is not in Thee! For as his joy

was unreal, so was my glory unreal; and it turned my brain even more. He would sleep off his drunkenness that very night: I had slept and risen, and was still to sleep and rise with mine—how many days? Yet there is a difference in the source of joy; I know it well, and the joy of faithful hope is worlds apart from vanity such as his; but at that time the beggar was better than I. For in truth he was the happier man, not only because he was steeped in jollity, while my life was torn out of me by anxiety, but also because he had chosen the right means and got his wine, while I was vainly seeking to feed pride with lies. Much I said to this effect to my friends, and I often saw in them how it was with myself. And I found that it was very ill with me, and by sorrow I doubled the ill. And, if good fortune smiled upon me, I was too sick at heart to catch at it; for, almost before I closed my hand, it flew away.

CHAPTER VII

How he converted Alypius from the madness of the Circus.

SUCH were our complaints who lived together as friends; but most frequently and most confidentially I used to open my troubles to Alypius and Nebridius. Alypius was a native of the same town as myself; his parents were burgesses of the best condition, but he was younger than I. For he had been one of my pupils when I first began to lecture in our town, and afterwards at Carthage, and he was warmly attached to me, through his opinion of my character and learning; so also was I to him, because of the virtuous excellence which was conspicuous in one so young. But at Carthage the foolish passion for public shows is like a boiling whirlpool; he too had been sucked in by the madness of the Circus. While he was tossing miserably in this gulf, I had already become professor of rhetoric there and kept a public school; but he did not as yet attach himself to my class, in consequence of a difference which had arisen between his father and myself. I had discovered that he was ruinously addicted to the Circus, and it was a deep grief to me, because I thought he was likely to ruin, if he had not already ruined, such fair hopes. But I could find no opportunity of admonishing or putting any pressure upon him, because I had neither the confidence of friendship nor the authority of a master. For I imagined that he regarded me with the same feelings as his father; but he did not. And so, disregarding his father's wishes in the matter, he began to salute me, and come to my lecture room, and listen for a while, and then go away. But in truth I had forgotten to remonstrate with him on the danger of marring so excellent a disposition by blind and reckless devotion to idle sports.

2. But Thou, O Lord, who standest by the helm of all things that Thou hast made, hadst

N

not forgotten that he was one day to be numbered among Thy sons, a priest of Thy sacrament; and, in order that his amendment might plainly be ascribed to Thee, Thou didst bring it about through my unconscious agency. For one day, when I was sitting in my accustomed place with all my scholars around me, he came, saluted me, took his seat, and applied his mind to the subject in hand. It so happened that I was busied with the exposition of a passage which suggested the use of the Circensian games as an illustration, enabling me to convey my meaning in a clearer and more attractive way, with a touch of sarcasm upon the victims of that mad folly. Thou knowest, O my God, that I was not thinking of curing Alypius of that plague. But he took my words home to himself, and thought that I had so spoken only on his account. And what would have made another angry with me, made that good lad angry with himself, and more devoted to me. For long ago Thou didst say and write it in Thy book: "Rebuke a wise man and he will love thee." [1]

3. Yet it was not I that had rebuked him; but Thou, who dost employ all men, whether they know it or not, as instruments in the plan that Thou hast designed—and that plan is just—didst make my heart and tongue as burning coals to cauterise and heal the wasting disease of that promising intelligence. Let him refuse to sing Thy praise who knoweth not Thy mercy, which makes confession unto Thee from my inmost

[1] Prov. ix. 8.

soul. For, moved by those words, Alypius leaped out of that deep pit into which he had wilfully plunged, and wherein he was blinded by a wretched passion; he shook his mind with a strong self-control, till all the mud of the Circus flew out of it, nor did he ever enter the place again. Moreover, he overcame the reluctance of his father, and obtained permission to join my class. The father gave way, and gave leave. And now Alypius, becoming once more my pupil, was entangled in my superstition, admiring the Manicheans for their profession of austerity, which he thought real and genuine. But in truth it was irrational and deceitful, lying in wait for precious souls unskilled as yet to fathom the depths of virtue, and therefore easy to beguile with the superficial charm of a shadowy and pretended virtue.

CHAPTER VIII

How Alypius was caught by the madness of gladiatorial shows, which he had formerly abhorred.

YET he did not abandon the earthly vocation which his parents had laid upon him as a spell, and so he had gone before me to Rome to be bred to the law. And there he was seized —is it not incredible?—with an incredible passion for gladiatorial shows. He hated and

abominated them, but a knot of friends and
fellow-students, happening to meet him in the
street as they were returning from breakfast,
dragged him with playful violence into the amphitheatre, in spite of his refusal and resistance, while
these cruel and bloody games were going on.
" If," cried he, " you drag my body thither, and
put me there, can you force me to give my mind
or my eyes to such a show? I shall be absent
in spirit, though present in body, and thus I shall
overcome both you and it." Nevertheless they
forced him to go along with them, being curious
perhaps to know whether he could do what he
said. They arrived and took their seats in the
best places they could find, at a moment when
the whole amphitheatre was raging with hideous
excitement.

2. He shut his eyes tight and forbade his
thoughts to dally with such crimes. Would he
could have sealed his ears also! For, at some turn
of the fight, the whole people broke into a roar
of shouting, and overcome by curiosity, confident
that whatever had happened he could despise and
forget even though he saw it, he opened his eyes.
Then was he struck with a deadlier wound in
his soul than the gladiator whom he lusted to
behold received in his flesh ; and fell more
miserably than the poor wretch over whose fall
arose that bellow which pierced his ears, and un-
locked his eyes, and laid open his soul to the
fatal thrust—his soul which was rash not brave,
and weak because it relied on its own strength,
when it should have relied on Thee. For, with

the sight of the blood, he drank in ruthlessness; no longer did he turn away, but fixed his gaze, and drained the cup of fury, and knew it not; he was fascinated by the sin of battle, and drunk with murderous joy. He was no longer the Alypius who had come, but one of the crowd to which he had come, and the hardened accomplice of those who had brought him! Why should I say more? He gazed, he shouted, he raved, he carried home with him a frenzy which goaded him to return, not only with those who at first had dragged him thither, but before them, dragging others in his turn. And yet with Thy strong and merciful hand Thou didst deliver him from thence, and didst teach him to trust, not in himself but in Thee, though not till long afterwards. But this event was stored up in his memory, to be a medicine for him in time to come.

CHAPTER IX

How Alypius was arrested as a thief.

THERE was another thing also which befell him, while he was yet a student, after he had joined my class at Carthage. One day at noon he was in the market hall, conning over the piece which he was to recite in class in the usual way, when Thou didst suffer him to be apprehended as a thief by the constables of the hall. And this, I

think, Thou didst permit, O my God, in order
that he, who was afterwards to be so great a
man, might thus early be taught that one human
being ought not to be condemned by another
hastily or with rash credulity. You must know
that he was walking up and down before the
tribunal, alone, with his tablets and style in his
hands, when, lo, one of the students, the real
thief, unperceived by Alypius, came in as far as
the leaden gratings which form the roof of the
silversmiths' booths, and began to cut away the
lead with an axe which he had brought beneath
his cloak. The sound of the axe caused an alarm
among the silversmiths beneath, and men were
sent to apprehend whomsoever they should find.
Hearing the outcry the thief made off, leaving
behind his weapon, lest he should be caught with
it in his hands.

2. Alypius, though he had not noticed the
man coming in, saw him go out in a very hurried
manner, and, curious to know what the reason
could be, walked to the spot, picked up the axe,
and was standing there looking at it; when, lo,
the officers came upon him, alone, and holding
the very axe which had made all the noise.
They seized him, and dragged him off amidst a
crowd of shopkeepers, who were full of joy at
having caught a thief in the act, and thence he
was to be carried before the magistrate. But
his lesson was to go no further. For immediately, O Lord, Thou didst come to the
rescue of his innocence, whereof Thou wast the
sole witness. As he was being led off to prison

or punishment, up came the architect of the public buildings. The captors rejoiced to meet the very official who had more than once suspected them of stealing goods that had been missed from the forum; now at last, they thought, he would see who was the real culprit.

3. But the architect had often met Alypius at the house of a senator, whose receptions he used to attend. He recognised him directly, and, taking his hand, led him apart from the throng, asked the cause of his misfortune, and learned what had occurred. Upon this he desired the bystanders to cease from their noise and threatenings, and come with him. So they went to the house of the student who had committed the crime. There was a slave-boy before the door, so young that the truth might easily be extracted from him, as he would not fear any harm to his master, whom he had attended to the forum. Alypius recognised him, and whispered to the architect, who showed the boy the axe and asked whose it was. "Ours," he answered immediately, and, being further questioned, disclosed the whole. So the guilt was shifted to that household, and, to the confusion of the mob who had already begun to triumph over him, the future steward of Thy word and judge of so many causes in Thy church went away home a wiser and more experienced man.

CHAPTER X

*The integrity of Alypius. The arrival of
Nebridius.*

HIM then I found at Rome, and he was bound
to me with hoops of steel, and went with me
to Milan, that he might not be deprived of my
society, hoping also to obtain some practice in
the law, which he had studied to please his
parents rather than himself.   There he had
already become Assessor, and showed an integrity which seemed strange to his brethren,
while he himself thought those strange who
preferred gold to honesty.   His virtue was
attempted not only with the lure of covetousness,
but with the goad of menace.   At Rome he
was Assessor to the Count of the Italian Bounty
Office.

2. There was at that time a very powerful
senator, to whom many were under obligation,
and whom many had reason to fear.   In his
usual high-handed way he desired to obtain some
decree in his favour, which the laws would not
allow ; Alypius refused the application ; a bribe
was offered ; he scorned it ; threats were used ;
he kicked against the pricks, so that all marvelled
at this rare spirit, which would not have the
friendship and did not fear the enmity of a
powerful man, who enjoyed a high reputation
because he could help or injure in a thousand

different ways. The very judge, whose assessor
he was, though he misliked the business, would
not openly refuse, but put the blame on Alypius,
alleging that he would not permit him to give his
assent, and in truth, if he had made the decree,
Alypius would have left the court. On one
occasion he was told that he might have books
copied for him at Government prices, and this
temptation, appealing as it did to his love of
letters, was almost too strong for him. But he
took counsel of justice, and changed his mind for
the better, thinking the scruple which forbade a
sounder rule to follow than the privilege which
allowed. This is a little matter, but he that is
faithful in little is faithful also in much. Nor
can that ever be void which was uttered by Thy
Truth : "If ye have not been faithful in the
unrighteous mammon, who will commit to your
trust the true riches? And if ye have not been
faithful in that which is another man's, who shall
give you that which is your own?"[1] Such was
Alypius, who then clave unto me, and with me
hesitated what manner of life to follow.

3. With me also was Nebridius, who had left
his native town near Carthage, and Carthage
itself, where he spent most of his time, and the
wealthy estate that had come to him from his
father, and his house, and his mother who would
not follow him, and had come to Milan for no
other reason than that he might live with me in
eager search after truth and wisdom. All my
sighs he echoed, and all my doubts he shared;

[1] Luke xvi. 10-12.

none sought so ardently for the blessed life, or pierced so keenly into the most difficult problems. Thus were we three famishing mouths, complaining of our distress one to another, and waiting upon Thee that Thou mightest give us our meat in due season.[1] In every vexation which in Thy mercy visited our worldly pursuits, we sought the reason why we suffered; and all was darkness; and we murmured and asked, " How long shall it be thus?" Often did we ask this, yet did we not forsake the way of the world, because as yet we could see no certain truth which we could grasp in its stead.

CHAPTER XI

Augustine deliberates anxiously on a change of life.

AND I especially mused and wondered when I remembered how long a time had passed since my nineteenth year, in which I first fell in love with wisdom, and determined, as soon as I could obtain her, to abandon the empty hopes and mad delusions of vain desires. And, lo, I was already thirty, still stuck fast in the same mire, still greedy of enjoying the present which fled from me and distracted me, still saying, "To-morrow I shall find; the truth will appear, and I shall grasp it;" or, "Lo, Faustus will come and explain everything." Or, "O ye sages of the

[1] Ps. cxlv. 15.

Academy, is there then no certainty that man can grasp for the guidance of life?" or, "Nay, let us seek more earnestly and never despair. Lo, I can already see that the things which seemed so absurd in the church's books are not absurd at all, and can be honestly understood in a different way. I will plant my feet firmly on that ground where my parents placed me, until the evident truth be discovered.

2. But where shall I seek it? when shall I seek it? Ambrose has no time to spare; I have no time to read. How am I to procure even the books? Whence or where can I obtain them? from whom can I borrow them? Let me plan out my time: let me set apart fixed hours for the salvation of my soul. The Catholic faith does not teach what I thought, what I vainly charged against her. Her doctors count it a sin to believe that God is bounded by the shape of a human body, and do I delay to knock that the rest also may be opened unto me?[1] My pupils take up the morning hours. What am I doing with the others? Why not this? But then, when am I to visit my great friends, whose influence I need? When am I to prepare the lectures I sell to my class? When am I to find refreshment, and relax my mind from the strain of work? Let everything go; away with this idle trifling; let me devote myself wholly to the search for truth! This life is wretched; death is certain. If it comes suddenly upon me, how shall I go hence, and where shall I learn

[1] Matt. vii. 7.

what here I have neglected? Nay, shall I not rather be doomed to suffer the punishment of my negligence here? But suppose death cuts off and finishes all care and feeling. This too must be looked into. But God forbid that it should be so. It is not for nothing, it is not in vain, that the stately authority of the Christian faith has overspread the world. Never would God have done so great things for us if the life of the soul perished with the death of the body. Why not, then, cast off the hopes of the world and give myself up, wholly and at once, to seeking after God and the blessed life?

3. Yet wait a little. This life also is pleasant, and has no small sweetness of its own. Nor is it a light matter to cut off the desire of the world, for it would be shameful to return to it again. See now, it is no very difficult matter to obtain some piece of preferment, and then what more should I desire? I have many powerful friends, if nothing else, and, if I push my claims, I may obtain even a governorship; then I can marry a wife with a little money, to help towards expenses, and that will be the limit of my desires. Many great men, worthy of all imitation, have combined the pursuit of wisdom with a married life."

4. While I talked like this and the wind kept shifting and driving my heart now hither now thither, time was slipping away; I delayed my conversion to the Lord; I adjourned from day to day the life in Thee, but daily death in myself I could not adjourn. I loved the blessed life, but feared

to seek it in its own abode; and I fled from it,
while I sought it. For I thought that I should
be miserable without the embraces of a woman.
I never gave a thought to the medicine which
Thy mercy has provided for the healing of that
infirmity, because I had never tested it, and
fancied that continence depended on our own
strength. Such strength I was conscious that I
did not possess, and in my folly I knew now how
it is written: "None can be continent unless
Thou give it." [1] Certainly Thou wouldest have
given it, if with unuttered groanings I had be-
sieged Thine ears, and with firm faith had cast
my care upon Thee.

CHAPTER XII

*Debate between Alypius and Augustine on
Marriage and Celibacy.*

IT was Alypius who prevented me from marry-
ing a wife, urging that, if I did so, it would
not be possible for us to live together in the
peaceful pursuit of wisdom, as we had long
desired to do. He himself, even at that time,
was a man of unblemished chastity; and this was
remarkable, because in the outset of his youth he
had actually made trial of sexual pleasure; but
it had not captivated him, rather he looked upon
it with shame and contempt, and from that time

[1] Wisdom viii. 21.

onwards lived in perfect continence. But I
quoted against him instances of men who had
been married, yet lovers of wisdom, and had
pleased God, and been loyal and affectionate to
their friends. Truly I was far inferior to them
in greatness of soul. Caught by the fatal sweetness of my carnal disease I dragged my chain,
and was afraid to be loosed : thus I rejected the
words of him that counselled wisely, as if the hand
that would have loosed me only hurt my wound.

2. Moreover, the serpent spoke by me to
Alypius, and twined enticing snares and laid them
in his way by the agency of my tongue, to catch
his upright and unencumbered feet. For he
wondered that I, for whom he had a great
esteem, should be caught so fast in the birdlime,
as to maintain, whenever we conversed upon the
subject, that I could not possibly live a single life.
And, when I defended myself against his wonder
by asserting that the hasty and stolen delight,
which he had tasted and now hardly remembered,
and therefore too hastily disparaged, was not to be
compared with a settled enjoyment such as mine,
and that, if to this settled enjoyment were added
the honourable name of marriage, I could not
think lightly of such a life, nor ought he to
wonder at me—·upon this, I say, he too began to
turn his thoughts towards wedlock, not that he
was overcome by the desire of pleasure, but out
of curiosity. For, he said, he longed to know
what that could be without which my life, which
he thought so happy, seemed to me to be no life
at all but a punishment.

3. For he, who carried no chain, was amazed at my slavery, and amazement awoke the desire for experience, from which he would have passed to the actual experience, and thence perhaps have fallen into the very slavery that amazed him, since he was minded to make a covenant with death,[1] and he that loves danger shall fall into it.[2] For neither of us gave any but the slightest heed to the honour of wedlock, such as it is, that is to say, to the duty of governing the wedded life and of bringing up children. As for me, it was mainly the strong habit of indulging an insatiate lust that bound and scourged me, while he was being dragged into slavery by mere wonder. In this state were we, until Thou, O most High, who never forsakest our clay, didst take pity on our misery and help us in ways wonderful and secret.

CHAPTER XIII

How a Wife was sought for Augustine.

AND I was being urgently pressed to marry. Already I was a suitor, already a bride was promised, and none was so eager as my mother. Her hope was that, as soon as I was married, I might be washed clean in saving baptism, for which she saw with joy that I was being daily prepared, and that her prayers and Thy promises

[1] Is. xxviii. 15.   [2] Ecclesiasticus iii. 26.

were on the point of fulfilment in my faith.   Yet
when, by my request and of her own impulse,
she called upon Thee daily with strong cries of
heart, that Thou wouldest discover to her in a
vision Thy purpose as to my marriage, Thou
wouldest never answer.

2. She saw indeed some vain creatures of the
imagination, such as are conjured up by the strong
preoccupation of the human spirit, and these she
related to me, but slightingly, and not with the
assurance that she used to have when Thou hadst
given her a revelation.   For she always said that
she could distinguish, by a certain feeling impossible to describe, between Thy revelations and
the dreams of her own soul.   Yet I was pressed,
and proposals were made for a girl, who was as
yet about two years too young to marry.   And
because she pleased me, I agreed to wait.

CHAPTER XIV

*How he proposed to live in common with a brother-
hood of friends.*

WITH a band of friends I had been discussing and deploring the stormy anxieties of
human life, and by this time we had almost de-
cided to live a peaceful life away from the crowd.
Peace we thought we might obtain by clubbing
together whatever means we possessed, and so
making one common stock; in the sincerity of

friendship there was to be no mine or thine, but
all were to have one purse and the whole was to
belong to each and all. We thought we might
reckon some ten members of this fraternity,
of whom some were very wealthy, especially
Romanianus, my fellow-townsman, whom at this
time pressing anxieties of business had brought up
to the Bounty Office. From childhood he had
been one of my nearest friends. He was the
warmest advocate of our project, and his words
carried great weight, because his wealth was
much greater than that of the others.

2. We had resolved that each year two of us
should be managers, and provide all that was
needful, while the others enjoyed complete
leisure. But as soon as we began to ask whether
the wives, whom some already had, and I hoped
to have, would tolerate this, our excellent plan
burst to pieces in our hands, and was cast aside
like a broken thing. Then our hearts turned to
sighs and groans, and our feet to the broad and
beaten track [1] of the world; for many thoughts
were in our heart, but Thy counsel standeth fast
for ever. [2] Strong in Thy counsel Thou didst
laugh at ours and pave the way for Thine own,
purposing to give us meat in due season, to open
Thy hand and fill our souls with blessing. [3]

[1] Matt. vii. 13.   [2] Ps. xxxiii. 11.
          [3] Ps. cxlv. 15, 16.

o

CHAPTER XV.

*How he took a second concubine in place
of the first.*

MEANWHILE my sins were being multiplied. My mistress was torn from my side as an obstacle to my marriage, and my heart, which clung to her, was torn and wounded till it bled. She had gone back to Africa, vowing unto Thee that she would never know any other man, leaving with me my natural son by her. But I, unhappy that I was, and weaker than a woman, could not bear the delay of two years which must elapse before I could obtain my promised bride, and so, being not a lover of wedlock but a slave of lust, I procured another mistress— I cannot call her wife—in order that under the guard of an unbroken custom the disease of my soul might be fed and carried on, as strong or stronger than ever, into the kingdom of a wife. Nor yet was the wound healed which had been caused by cutting away my former love ; only it ceased to burn and throb, and began to fester, and was more dangerous because less painful.

CHAPTER XVI.

How he never lost the fear of death and judgment.

THINE is the praise, Thine the glory, O Thou fount of mercies. I was more wretched, and Thou wast closer. Nearer and nearer came Thy right hand, to pluck me out of the mire and rescue me, and I knew it not. Nor did anything call me back from a deeper pit of carnal pleasures but the fear of death and of Thy judgment to come, which, throughout all the changes of my opinions, never faded from my breast. And I discussed with my friends Alypius and Nebridius the nature of Good and Evil, maintaining that in my judgment Epicurus would have carried off the palm, unless I had believed, what Epicurus did not believe, that the life of the soul, and the requital of good or ill desert, endure after death.

2. And, putting the case that we were immortal and lived in the unbroken enjoyment of bodily pleasure without any fear of losing it, I asked why we should not be happy, or what else we could desire. I did not know that this was in fact the root of my misery, that I was so fallen and blinded that I could not discern the light of virtue and of beauty, which must be embraced for its own sake, which the eye of flesh cannot see, and only the inner vision can see. Nor did I

consider, alas! the reason why I found delight in discussing these very perplexities, shameful as they were, with my friends, or why I could not be happy without my friends, even according to the notions of happiness which I then cherished, however rich the store of my carnal pleasures might be. Yet certainly I loved my friends for their own sakes, and felt that they in turn loved me for my own sake.

3. O what crooked paths! Woe to the rash soul which hopes by forsaking Thee to find something better. It tosses and turns upon back and side and belly; but the bed is hard, and Thou alone art rest. And, lo! thou art near, and settest free from the misery of wandering, and plantest our feet in Thy road, and comfortest us, saying, "Run, I will carry you, and I will bring you home, and then I will set you free."

BOOK VII

HE recalls the beginning of his man-
hood, that is to say, the thirty-
first year of his age. He tells
how at that time the darkness of
his ignorance was thicker than
ever, and how through many
errors about the nature of God,
and much grievous perplexity
about the origin of Evil, he
attained at last to a sound knowledge of God, though as yet he
held unworthy opinions about the
Lord Christ.

CHAPTER I.

He thinks of God as a corporeal entity diffused through infinite space.

BY this time my evil and shameful youth was dead; I was entering upon middle age, and as my years increased so did my levity. I could conceive of no substance except visible; yet I no longer thought of Thee, O God, under the form of a human body. Ever since I inclined my ear to philosophy I avoided this error; and the truth on this point I rejoiced to find in the faith of our spiritual mother, Thy Catholic Church. Yet could I not see what else to think of Thee. Man as I was, and such a man as I was, I strove to form a conception of Thee, the supreme and one and true God. With all my heart I believed that Thou wast incorruptible, inviolable, unchangeable, because, though I knew not how or why, I yet discerned plainly and beyond a doubt that the corruptible is worse than the incorruptible, the inviolable obviously superior to its opposite, the unchangeable better than the changeable.

2. My heart protested strongly against all my phantasms, and with this one certainty I endeavoured to brush away the swarm of unclean flies

that hovered around the eyes of my mind.   But in a moment they gathered again, beat against my face, and clouded my vision.   I no longer thought of God in a human body, yet some kind of body I was constrained to imagine, reaching through space, permeating the world, or diffused through infinity outside the world, and this was the incorruptible, inviolable, unchangeable substance which I thought better than the corruptible, violable, changeable.   For, whatever I deprived of the dimensions of space appeared to me to be nothing —absolutely nothing, not even a void.   For if a body is taken out of space, and that portion of space is emptied of all its contents, of earth, water, air, or heaven, yet there remains an empty space, a measurable nothing.

3. So gross then were my ideas that, though I could not see my own self, I held that whatever had neither length nor breadth nor density nor solidity, and did not, or could not, acquire such attributes, was absolutely nothing.   For at that time my mind dwelt only with ideas resembling the forms with which my eyes are still familiar, nor could I see that the act of thought by which I formed those ideas was itself immaterial ; I held that it could not have formed the ideas unless it were a measurable thing.   So also I thought of Thee, O Life of my life, as stretched out through infinite spaces, interpenetrating the whole mass of the world, reaching out beyond in all directions to immensity without end, so that sea, sky, all things are full of Thee, limited in Thee while Thou art not limited at all.

4. As the body of the air above the earth does not bar the passage of the light of the sun, but the light penetrates the air, not bursting or dividing it, but filling it, in the same way, I thought, the body of heaven, and air, and sea, and even of earth was all pervious to Thee, penetrable in all its parts great or small, so that it can admit the secret inspiration of Thy presence, which from within or from without orders all things that Thou hast created. This was my fancy, for I could shape no other; yet it was false. For in that way a greater part of the earth would contain a greater part of Thee, a less part a less. All things would be full of Thee in such a sense that there would be more of Thee in the elephant than in the sparrow, inasmuch as one is larger than the other, and fills a wider space. And thus Thou wouldest unite Thy limbs piecemeal with the limbs of the world, the great with the great, the small with the small. This is not Thy nature; but as yet Thou hadst not lightened my darkness.

CHAPTER II

The argument with which Nebridius used to confute the Manicheans.

I HAD a sufficient answer, O Lord, against those deceived deceivers, those dumb praters —dumb because Thy word did not sound forth from them—I say I had a sufficient answer,

which in the old Carthaginian days Nebridius
used to urge, shaking all of us who heard it.
"What could this imaginary people of darkness,
which the Manichees set in battle array against
Thee, have done to Thee, if Thou hadst declined
the combat?" If they replied that it could have
hurt Thee, they would have made Thee violable
and corruptible. If, on the other hand, it could
have done Thee no harm, then there was no
cause for any battle at all, far less for such a
battle, in which a part of Thee, a member of
Thee, a child of Thy own substance, was mixed
up with adverse powers not of Thy creation, and
by them corrupted and deteriorated and changed
from happiness into misery, so that it could not
be delivered and cleansed without Thy help.
And this child is the soul, and Thy Word
which is to help it in its slavery, its impurity, its
corruption, must needs be free, pure, incorrupt.
Yet by the hypothesis the Word is itself corrupt,
because of one and the same substance as the soul.

2. And therefore, if they admitted that Thy
nature, the substance whereby Thou art, is
incorruptible, their whole theory must be false
and abominable. But if they regarded Thee as
corruptible, that is false to start with, and should
be rejected with horror as soon as uttered.
This, I say, was a sufficient answer against these
deceivers, who ought to be spued forth by the
men whom they have surfeited; for out of this
dilemma they could find no way of escape, without dreadful sacrilege of mind and tongue, so
long as they think and speak these things of Thee.

CHAPTER III

That freewill is the cause of sin.

BUT as yet, though I affirmed and strongly believed that Thou, O Lord, the true God, who didst create not only our souls but our bodies, and not only our souls and bodies but the whole universe, wast free from stain or alteration or any shadow of change, nevertheless I could not grasp clearly and intelligibly the cause of evil. But, whatever it was, I saw that I must not accept any solution that would constrain me to attribute mutability to the immutable God, lest I should become the very thing which I was investigating. And so I pursued the search with a quiet mind, feeling now confident that what was said by the Manicheans, whom I shrank from with my whole heart, could not be true, because I perceived that, when they asked what wos the origin of evil, the answer was dictated by a wicked pride, which would rather affirm Thy nature to be capable of suffering evil than their own nature of doing it. And I tried hard to see, what now I was told, that the freedom of the will is the cause of our doing ill, and that Thy just judgment is the cause of our suffering ill. But I could not see this clearly.

2. And so, when I strove to lift up my mental vision out of that deep pit, I fell back again; often did I strive, and again and again

did I fall back. One thing lifted me up towards Thy light; it was that I had come to know that I had a will, as certainly as I knew that I was alive. And so, when I willed to do or not to do anything, I was absolutely sure that I, and not somebody else, willed it; and I was beginning to perceive that there lay the cause of my sin. What I did against my will, I could see that I suffered rather than did, and such actions I looked upon not as faults but as punishments, which I soon confessed were well deserved, because I could not but feel that Thou art just.

3. But again I asked, Who made me? Was it not my God, who is not only good, but the Good? How did I come then to will evil and not to will good, so that there should be a just reason for my punishment? Who set this in me, who planted in me a root of bitterness, when I was altogether the handiwork of my most sweet God? If the devil is to blame, who made the devil himself? And, if he was a good angel who by his own wicked will became the devil, how did there happen to be in him that wicked will by which he became a devil, since a good Creator made him wholly a good angel? By these thoughts I was beaten down again and suffocated. Yet I did not fall again into that hell of error where no man confesseth unto Thee, wherein Thou art thought to suffer ill, rather than man to do it.

CHAPTER IV

That God must be incorruptible.

FOR, in my endeavours to solve my remaining perplexities, I assumed henceforth as truth that the incorruptible is better than the corruptible ; and therefore I acknowledged that, whatever Thy nature might be, Thou wast incorruptible. For no soul ever has devised, or ever will devise, anything better than Thee who art the chief and best Good. And since beyond the shadow of a doubt the incorruptible is to be placed above the corruptible (as I did now admit) it followed that I could rise in my thought to something better than my God, if Thou wast not incorruptible. As soon then as I saw that the incorruptible was to be set above the corruptible, I was bound to seek Thee there, and from that starting-point to study the origin of evil, that is to say, of corruption, by which Thy substance cannot possibly be violated.

2. For certainly it is impossible that corruption should pollute our God, whether by choice or by necessity or by surprise, because He is God, and what He wills is good, and He is that same good. But to be corrupted is not good. Nor art Thou compelled to do anything against Thy will, because Thy will is not greater than Thy power. It could not be greater, unless Thou

wast greater than Thyself, for the will and power
of God are God Himself.   And what can take
Thee by surprise, since Thou knowest all, and
there is no nature except by reason of Thy
knowing it ?   But why should I heap up words
to prove that the substance which is God cannot
be corruptible ? for if it were so, He would not
be God.

CHAPTER V

Again he asks whence comes evil, and what is its
root.

I SOUGHT whence came ill, and I sought it
   ill, and saw not the ill that lurked in my
search.   I marshalled before the sight of my
spirit all creation, all that we see, earth, and sea,
and air, and stars, and trees, and animals ; all
that we do not see, the firmament of the sky
above, and all angels, and all spiritual things,
for these also, as if they were bodies, did my
imagination arrange in this place or in that.   I
pictured to myself Thy creation as one vast mass,
composed of various kinds of bodies, some real
bodies, some those which I imagined in place of
spirits.   I pictured this mass as vast, not indeed
in its true dimensions, for these I could not know,
but as large as I chose to think, only finite on
every side.   And Thee, O Lord, I conceived
as lapping it round and interpenetrating it everywhere, but as infinite in every direction ; as

if there were sea everywhere, and everywhere through measureless space nothing but illimitable sea, and within this sea a sponge, huge but yet finite ; the sponge would be pervaded through all its particles by the infinite sea.[1]   In this way I pictured Thy finite creation, as filled with Thy infinity, and I said to myself, " Behold God, behold God's creation ; God is good, eternally and immensely better than His works ; but as He is good so are His works good, and behold how He embraces and fills them all."

2. Where then is evil, and whence, and by what cranny did it make its origin ?   What is is root, and what is its seed ?   Or are we to think that it is not !   Why then do we fear it and shun it, if it is not ?   For even if our fear is groundless, yet that fear itself is evil, which stabs and tortures the heart for nothing.   Yes, it is all the more evil if there is nothing to fear, and yet we do fear.   Either then it is evil that we fear, or the fear itself is evil.   Whence then does it spring, seeing that the good God made all things good ?   It is true that He is the greater and sovereign Good, and that His works are lesser goods, yet Creator and creature are good alike.   Whence comes evil ?   Did He make His works of some evil matter, which He shaped and ordered, yet so as to leave behind a residuum which he could not turn into good ?   Then why

[1] Augustine's simile of the sponge in the infinite sea resembles, but is apparently not suggested by, the Plotinian simile of the Net in the water, *Enn.* iv. 3. 9.   Augustine's views were still quite materialistic.

was that? Had He not the power to alter and change the whole, so that no evil should be left, seeing that He is Almighty? Lastly, why did He choose to make anything of such stuff, why did He not rather annihilate it by the same almighty power? Could it exist against His will? Or, if it was eternal, why did He leave it unemployed through the infinite ages of the past, and then determine to make something out of it?

3. Supposing that He suddenly determined to act, would not an Almighty Being have chosen to abolish this tainted substance and live by Himself, the perfect, true, sovereign, and infinite Good? Or, if it was not good that He who was good should not fashion and establish something good, would He not have destroyed the evil matter and made a good one for the purpose of His creation? He would not be almighty, if He could not create good without help from a matter which He had not created. These doubts I pondered in my wretched breast, and what added poignancy to my distress was that I feared to die before I should have discovered the truth And yet the faith of Thy Christ, our Lord and Saviour, taught me by the Catholic Church, stuck fast in my heart. As yet it was shapeless and wandered from the straight line of doctrine, nevertheless my mind never lost hold upon it, but drank it in daily more and more.

CHAPTER VI

He rejects Astrology.

BY this time also I had renounced the lying
divinations and impious ravings of the astrologers. Here also let Thy mercies confess unto
Thee from the inmost recesses of my soul, O my
God. For Thou—beyond a doubt it was Thou,
(for who else calls us back from the Death of
every error, except the Life which never dies
and the Wisdom which, needing no light itself,
shines upon our needy souls, which governs the
whole world down to the leaves that flutter on
the trees?)—Thou didst provide a cure for the
stubbornness with which I resisted that sagacious
old man Vindicianus, and that admirable young
man Nebridius, of whom the former positively,
the latter with some hesitation, but repeatedly,
affirmed that there was no art of divination, but
that as oracles often turn out true, so it was with
the guesses of astrologers; for out of a great
number many will come to pass, though the men
who hazard them know nothing, and only stumble
on the truth by not saying nothing. Thou
didst provide, I say, a cure in the person of a
friend who had been a regular customer of the
astrologers. He was not a man of mature years,
nor had he studied the cabbalistic books, but, as
I say, he had been a regular customer. Yet he
knew some facts which, he said, he had learned

P

from his father, though he could not tell how far they might go towards destroying the reputation of the art.

2. Firminus, for that was his name, had received a liberal education and was a cultivated rhetorician, and it so happened that he consulted me, as his dearest friend, about some worldly affair, of which he had high expectations, asking me in particular how it fitted with his horoscope, as they call it. Though I had already begun to incline to the opinion of Nebridius, I did not actually refuse to make a forecast, nor did I explain to him my doubts, but said that I was almost convinced that astrology was mere nonsense. Upon this he told me that his father had been a diligent reader of astrological books, and had had a friend who pursued the subject with him with equal zeal. These two, he said, by common study and frequent converse, fanned the flame of their absurdity to such a height, that they would even record the minute of the birth of the dumb creatures about their houses, and cast their horoscopes, in order to collect observations in this so-called art.

3. "And so," Firminus said, "my father told me that, when my mother was expecting to be brought to bed of me, a female slave of his friend was also great with child, and this of course was known to her master, who used to register with the minutest care even the birth of his puppies. But while they were counting with laborious accuracy the days, hours and minutes, the one for his wife, the other for his bondwoman,

it so fell out that both women were delivered
at the same moment, so that they were compelled to make the same horoscope, down to the
minutest particulars, for the son and for the baby
slave.   For when the labour began, they sent
word to each other what was going on in their
respective houses; they got ready messengers to
despatch to each other as soon as they should be
informed of the actual birth, and made arrangements, each in his own domain, to be informed
of this, without a moment's delay.   Now these
messengers crossed one another so exactly in the
centre between the two houses, that neither could
mark the least difference in the position of the
stars or the natal influences.   And yet I," said
Firminus, "was born in a good position, advanced
rapidly along the sunny paths of the world, grew
in wealth, rose in rank; while that slave, as I was
told by one who knew him, remained just what
he was, without any relaxation of his yoke."

4.   When I heard this tale and believed it, for
the narrator was a man to be believed, all my
doubts were swept away.   Immediately I endeavoured to reclaim Firminus himself from his
superstition.   "When I set up your constellations," I said, "I could not have given a true
answer unless I had been able to read in them
that your parents were people of good position,
that your family was noble in its own city, that
your birth was free, your breeding gentle, your
education liberal.   But if that slave had consulted
me about these same constellations, for they were
his also, I could not have given him a true

answer, unless I had been able to read in them
a mean family, a servile condition, and so on, all
in direct contradiction to the former interpretation. Now how is it that I must draw a different
conclusion from the same facts, if I am to be
right? Yet, if I drew the same conclusion, I
should be altogether wrong." Hence I gathered
beyond a doubt that, when those who profess to
read the constellations hit the mark, their success
is due not to skill but to chance, and that, when
they miss, their failure is due not to imperfect
skill but to the deceitfulness of chance.

5. The way being thus made plain, I longed,
without loss of a moment, to fly upon the lunatics
who follow this base trade, and expose them to
universal derision. But they might reply that
I had been wrongly informed by Firminus, or
that Firminus had been deceived by his father.
Hence I fell to ruminating of the matter, and
bent my thoughts to the case of those who are
born twins. For generally they come forth
from the womb so immediately after one another
that the interval, whatever importance they may
ascribe to it in the nature of things, cannot be
appreciated by human observation, and certainly
cannot be noted down in the scheme of the constellations, which the astrologer must read before
he can rightly predict. And his prediction
cannot be right, because, after reading the same
scheme, he ought to tell the same fortune
for Esau and Jacob. But the history of
the two was not the same; so that he would
have been utterly wrong. Or, if he was right,

then he must have read different fortunes in the
same scheme. He would have been right then,
not by skill but by chance. For Thou, O Lord,
Thou most righteous Governor of the Universe,
dost so work by secret unconscious impulses
upon adept and enquirer alike, that each hears
what it is fitting that he should hear, according
to the hidden deserts of his soul and the deep
workings of Thy righteous judgment. To
which let no man say, "What is this?" or
"Why is this?" O say it not, say it not; for
thou art but man.

CHAPTER VII

*The question of the Origin of Evil causes him
great anguish of mind.*

ALREADY, O my Helper, Thou hadst
freed me from these fetters, and now I
was asking whence came evil, and could find no
road. But Thou didst not suffer the waves of
doubt to wash me away from my belief that
Thou art; that Thy substance is unchangeable;
that Thou takest thought for men and wilt
judge them; that Thou hast placed the way
of salvation, the way to the life after death, in
Christ, Thy Son, our Lord, and in the Holy
Scriptures, which the authority of Thy Catholic
Church guarantees. These were my axioms,
firmly rooted in my mind, and now I went on to
ask with feverish eagerness whence came evil. O

my God, with what anguish, with what groans did my heart travail to bring forth. And Thy ears were listening, though I knew not. And when I sought an answer silently with all my strength, the unspoken contrition of my soul appealed with loud cries to Thy mercy.

2. No man knew, but Thou knewest, what I was suffering. How little of it could I express in words to the ears of my dearest friends! How could the whole tumult of my soul, for which I had neither time nor utterance, be conveyed to them? But it was all poured into Thy ears, while I roared by reason of the disquietness of my heart, and my desire was before Thee, and the light of mine eyes was not with me.[1] For it was in Thee, and I was outside. Nor was that light in place; but I was thinking only of things that are contained in place, and could find in them no place to rest in; they did not welcome me, so that I could say "It is enough, it is well," nor did they let me go, so that I could reach what was enough and well. For I was higher than they, though lower than Thou; and Thou art my true joy, if I depend upon Thee; and Thou hadst subjected to me what Thou didst create inferior to me.

3. And this was the golden mean, the middle path of my salvation, to abide in Thy image, to rule my body and serve Thee. But when I behaved myself proudly against Thee, and ran against the Lord with the stiff neck of my

[1] Ps. xxxviii. 9, 10.

buckler,[1] even those lower things became a heavy weight above me, and crushed me down, so that there was no respite or time for breathing. They met my eyes on all sides, in troops and solid masses, and, when I tried to think, the images of bodies barred my escape, seeming to cry to me, " Whither goest thou, unworthy and unclean?" All this grew out of my wound, for Thou hast humbled the haughty as one that is wounded,[2] and by my swelling pride I was separated from Thee, and my puffed-out face closed up my eyes.

CHAPTER VIII.

How the Divine Pity succoured Augustine.

BUT Thou, O Lord, abidest for ever, and wilt not be angry with us for ever,[3] for Thou hast pity on us who are but dust and ashes; and Thou wast pleased to shape anew my unshapeliness in Thy sight. And Thou wast driving me on with Thy goad, so that I could not be at rest, until Thou wast manifest to the eye of my soul. Thus did all my swelling subside beneath the secret touch of Thy healing hand, and my perplexed and darkened sight was daily being healed by the mordant salve of wholesome grief.

[1] Job xv. 26 differing from both the English and the Vulgate.

[2] Ps. lxxxix. 10 agreeing with Ps. lxxxviii. 11 of the Vulgate.

[3] Pss. cii. 13; lxxxv. 5.

CHAPTER IX.

How in the Platonic Books he found the divinity of the Eternal Word, but not the humility of the Incarnate Word.

AND first of all, willing to teach me how Thou dost resist the proud and givest grace to the humble,[1] and how mercifully Thou hast made known to men the way of humility, in that Thy Word was made flesh and dwelt among men, Thou didst procure for me, through the agency of one puffed up with enormous vanity, certain books of the Platonists translated from the Greek into Latin. And therein I found, not indeed these precise words, but precisely the same truth fortified with many and divers arguments, that "in the beginning was the Word, and the Word was with God, and the Word was God, and the same was in the beginning with God; all things were made by Him, and without Him was nothing made that was made; in Him is life, and the life was the light of men, and the light shineth in darkness, and the darkness comprehended it not."[2] Further, that the soul of man, though it bears witness to the light, is not itself that light, but God, the Word of God, is the true light that lighteth every man that cometh into the world. And that "He was in the world, and the world was made by Him, and the world knew him not." But that "He came

[1] 1 Peter v. 5.   [2] John i. 1-12.

unto his own, and His own received Him not ;
but as many as received Him, to them gave He
power to become the sons of God, even to them
that believe on His name,"—this I could not
find there.

2. Also I found there that God the Word
" was born, not of flesh, nor of blood, nor of the
will of a man,[1] nor of the will of the flesh, but of
God." But that "the Word was made flesh
and dwelt among us," this I found not there.
I could discover in these books, though it was
expressed in other and in varying phrases, that
" the Son was in the form of the Father, and
thought it not robbery to be equal with God,"
because by nature He was that same substance.
But that " He emptied Himself, taking upon
Him the form of a servant, being made in the
likeness of men ; and, being found in fashion as a
man, He humbled Himself, and became obedient
unto death, even the death of the Cross ; wherefore also God exalted Him from the dead, and
gave Him a Name, which is above every name ;
that at the name of Jesus every knee should bow,
of things in heaven, and things in earth, and
things under the earth, and that every tongue
should confess that the Lord Jesus Christ is in
the glory of God the Father "[2]—this those
books do not contain.

[1] *non ex voluntate viri* (ἐκ θελήματος ἀνδρός, John i.
13) surely means "of the will of a man," "of the will
of a husband." But the Revised Version of the English
still reads "of the will of man."

[2] Phil. ii. 5-11. The Vulgate has *in gloria est Dei
Patris*.

3. For that, before all times and above all times, Thy only begotten Son abideth unchangeable and co-eternal with Thee, and that of His fullness all souls receive, in order that they may be blessed, and that by participation of the eternal wisdom they are renewed, in order that they may be wise, this is there.   But that in due time He died for the ungodly,[1] that Thou sparedst not Thine Only Son but deliveredst Him up for us all,[2] this is not there.   For Thou hast hidden these things from the wise, and revealed them unto babes, that they that labour and are heavy laden might come unto Him, and He might refresh them, because He is meek and lowly in heart,[3] and the meek He guideth in judgment, and the gentle He teacheth His ways,[4] looking upon our lowliness and troubles, and forgiving all our sins.[5]   But those who strut in the buskin of what they deem higher knowledge, will not listen to Him who saith, "Learn of me, for I am meek and lowly in heart, and ye shall find rest unto your souls," [6] and though they know God, yet they glorify Him not as God, nor are thankful, but become vain in their imaginations, and their foolish heart is darkened ; professing themselves to be wise, they became fools.[7]

4. And therefore, as I read there also, they had changed the glory of Thy incorruptible nature into idols and many kinds of images, into the likeness of the image of corruptible man, and

---

[1] Rom. v. 6.   [2] Rom. viii. 32.
[3] Matt. xi. 25, 28, 29.   [4] Ps. xxv. 9.
[5] Ps. xxv. 18.   [6] Matt. xi. 29.   [7] Rom. i. 21, 22.

birds, and four-footed beasts and creeping things,[1]
to wit, that flesh of Egypt for which Esau lost
his birthright; for Thy first-born people worshipped the head of a beast instead of Thee,
turning in heart back towards Egypt, and bowing down their soul, Thy likeness, before the
likeness of a calf that eateth hay.[2] These things
found I there, but I would not eat of them.
For it pleased Thee, O Lord, to take away the
reproach of inferiority from Jacob that the elder
should serve the younger,[3] and Thou calledst the
Gentiles into Thine inheritance.

5. And I had come to Thee from the Gentiles; and my mind was set upon the gold which
Thou willedst Thy people to carry off from
Egypt, for it was Thine wherever it was.[4] And
Thou didst say unto the Athenians by the mouth
of Thy Apostles that in Thee we live and move
and have our being, as certain also of their own
poets have said.[5] And surely these books came
from thence. But my mind was not set on the
idols of the Egyptians, which they fashioned of
Thy gold, changing the truth of God into a lie,
and worshipping and serving the creature more
than the Creator.[6]

---

[1] Rom. i. 23.   [2] Ps. cvi. 20.   [3] Rom. ix. 12.
[4] Perhaps Augustine has here in view a passage in
Origen's *Epistle to Gregory* § 2 (Lom. i. p. 2), where
also philosophy is compared to the gold borrowed by
the Israelites from the Egyptian.
[5] Acts xvii. 28.   [6] Rom. i. 15.

CHAPTER X

Augustine begins more clearly to discern divine Truth.

AND, being by these books admonished to
return into myself, I entered into the secret
closet of my soul, guided by Thee; and this I
could do because Thou wast my helper. I
entered, and beheld with the mysterious eye of
my soul the light that never changes, above the
eye of my soul, above my intelligence. It was
not the common light which all flesh can see, nor
was it greater yet of the same kind, as if the
light of day were to grow brighter and brighter
and flood all space. It was not like this, but
something altogether different from any earthly
illumination. Nor was it above my intelligence
in the same way as oil is above water, or heaven
above earth, but it was higher because it made
me, and I was lower because made by it. He
who knows the truth knows that Light, and he
who knows that Light knows Eternity. Love
knows that Light.

2. O eternal Truth, and true Love, and
lovely Eternity, Thou art my God; unto Thee
do I sigh night and day. When first I knew
Thee, Thou didst take hold of me, so that I
could see there was something to be seen, though
I was not yet fit to see it. And Thou didst
beat back my weak sight, dazzling me with Thy

splendour, and I thrilled with love and dread, and I perceived that I was far away from Thee in the land of unlikeness, as if I heard Thy voice from on high crying unto me, " I am the Food of the full-grown ; become a man, and Thou shalt feed on me. Nor shalt Thou change Me into thine own substance, as thou changest the food of thy flesh, but thou shalt be changed into Mine." And I understood that Thou dost chasten man for iniquity, and hast made my soul to consume away like a spider's web.[1] And I said, " Is truth, then, nothing, because it is not diffused through space finite or infinite?" And Thou didst cry from afar, " Nay, not so; I AM THAT I AM." And I heard as the heart heareth, and there was left no room for doubt. Sooner could I doubt my own existence than think that Truth is not, for it is clearly seen and understood by means of the things which are made.[2]

CHAPTER XI

How the creatures are and are not.

AND I beheld all the things that are beneath Thee, and I saw that they are neither wholly real nor wholly unreal ; they are real in so far as they came from Thee, they are unreal

[1] Ps. xxxix. 11, agreeing with xxxviii. 12 of the Vulgate. [2] Rom. i. 20.

because they are not what Thou art. For that alone is truly real which abides unchanged. It is good then for me to hold me fast by God,[1] because if I abide not in Him, I cannot abide in myself. But He, abiding in Himself, maketh all things new.[2] And Thou art the Lord my God, because my goods are nothing unto Thee.[3]

CHAPTER XII

All that is, is Good.

AND it was made clear to me that all things that are corrupted are good. They could not be corrupted, if they were chief goods, nor unless they were goods; because, if they were chief goods, they would be incorruptible, and if they were not goods at all, there would be nothing in them that could be corrupted. For corruption does harm, and it can do harm only by diminishing goodness. Either then corruption does no harm, which is impossible, or all things that are corrupted are deprived of good, and this is most certainly true. But, if they are deprived of all good, they will cease to exist. For, if they exist and can be no further corrupted, they will be better because henceforth they remain incorruptible.

2. Now what can be more monstrous than

[1] Ps. lxxiii. 28.   [2] Wisdom vii. 27.
[3] Ps. xvi. 2.

to maintain that, by losing all good, they have become better. If then they are deprived of all good, they will cease to exist. Therefore, so long as they exist, they are good. Therefore, all that exists is good. And so that evil, whose origin I was seeking, is not a substance; because, if it were a substance, it would be good. For either it would be an incorruptible substance, that is to say, a chief good, or a corruptible substance, which could not be corrupted unless it were good. And so I saw, and saw clearly that all that Thou hast made is good; and there are no substances at all which Thou didst not make. And because Thou didst not make all things equal, each by itself is good, and the sum of all is very good; for our God made all things very good.[1]

CHAPTER XIII

All creation praises God.

AND to Thee there is no such thing as evil, and even to Thy creation as a whole there is not, because there is nothing beyond it that can burst in and destroy the law which Thou

[1] Individual things are good; the whole is very good. The whole likeness of God is found in the whole world, partial likeness in the several parts. This interpretation of Gen. i. 31, was taken from St Augustine by St Thomas Aquinas, and is finely developed in the *Summa Contra Gentiles*, ii 44

hast imposed upon it. In the details there are things which, because they suit not some parts, are counted evil, yet these same things suit other parts, and are good to them, and are good in themselves. And all these things which are not suitable to one another, are yet suitable to that lower half of creation called earth, which has its own windy and cloudy sky of like nature with itself.

2. What folly, then, would it be to think that nothing exists except this world of sense. For, if I saw this world alone, I should long indeed for a better, yet should I be bound to praise Thee for this world alone. For, that Thou art to be praised on earth, the dragons do show and all deeps, fire, hail, snow, ice and stormy wind fulfilling Thy word; mountains and all hills, fruitful trees and all cedars; beasts and all cattle, creeping things and feathered fowl; kings of the earth and all people, princes and all judges of the earth; young men and maidens, old men and children praise Thy Name. But seeing that in heaven all Thy angels praise Thee, praise Thee, O God, in the height, and all Thy hosts, sun and moon, all stars and light, the heaven of heavens and the waters that be above the heavens praise Thy Name,[1] seeing this, I say, I no longer desired a better world, because my thought ranged over all, and with a sounder judgment I reckoned that things above were better than things below, yet that all creation together was better than the things above.

[1] Ps. cxlviii. 1-12.

CHAPTER XIV

The sane mind finds nothing evil in God's creation.

THERE is no health in those who find fault with any part of Thy creation, as there was no health in me, when I found fault with many of Thy works. And, because my soul did not dare to find fault with God, it denied that the faults it found were Thy handiwork. Thus it had wandered into the notion of two substances, and could find no rest, and talked a strange language. And, escaping from that error, it had made for itself a God extended through infinite space, and thought it to be Thee, and set it up in its heart, and became once more the temple of its own idol, abominable in Thy sight. But Thou didst soothe my brain, though I knew it not, and closed my eyes lest they should behold vanity,[1] and thus by slow degrees my folly ceased and fell asleep. And I awoke in Thee and beheld Thee infinite, yet not in such a manner as I had supposed, and this vision was not derived from the flesh.

[1] Ps. cxix. 37.

CHAPTER XV

*How there is Truth and Falsehood in
Creation.*

AND I looked upon other things, and I saw
that all that is finite owes to Thee its
existence in Thee ; yet it is in Thee not as it is
in space, but because Thou holdest all things in
the hand of Thy truth : and that all things are
true in so far as they are ; and that falsehood is
nothing, except the existence in thought of that
which is not.   And I saw that everything bears
fit relation, not only to its place but to its time ;
and that Thou, who alone art Eternal, didst not
begin to work after the lapse of innumerable
ages, because no time, either of past or of future,
could come or go, except by Thy working and
abiding.

CHAPTER XVI

*How all that is created is good, though it may not
suit everything.*

AND I felt and realised that it is nothing
strange, if bread, which is sweet, is a
punishment to the diseased palate, and light,
which is lovely to healthy eyes, is hateful to
the sick.   And the wicked find fault with Thy

justice, as they do with the viper and the worm,
yet these are good, though belonging only to the
lower order of Thy creation. And there is
the proper place of the wicked also, the more
unlike they are to Thee; yet do they belong
also to the higher order, the more they become
like Thee. And I asked what wickedness was,
and I found that it was no substance, but a perversity of will, which turns aside from Thee, O
God, the supreme substance, to desire the lowest,
flinging away its inner treasure [1] and boasting
itself an outcast.

CHAPTER XVII

*What it is that holds man back from the knowledge
of the Divine.*

AND I marvelled to find that now I loved
Thee, and not a phantasm in Thy stead.
And I could not stand still to enjoy my God,
but was swept up to Thee by Thy beauty, and
again torn away from Thee by my own weight,[2]
and fell back with a groan into the world of
sense; and the weight was carnal use and wont.
But Thy memory dwelt with me, nor did I
doubt in the least that there was One for me to

[1] Ecclesiasticus x. 10 (Vulgate), *quoniam in vita sua
proiecit intima sua.* The R.V. has *because in his life he hath
cast away his bowels.*

[2] Wisdom ix. 15.

cleave to, only I doubted whether I was as yet able to cleave to Him, forasmuch as the corruptible body presseth down the soul, and the earthly tabernacle weigheth down the mind that museth upon many things.[1] Most certain I was that Thy invisible things are clearly seen from the constitution of the world, being understood through the things that are made, even Thy eternal power and Godhead.[2]

2. For when I asked how I could estimate the beauty of bodies, whether celestial or terrestrial, and what rule was ready to my hand so that I could judge correctly of changeable things and say This ought to be thus, that ought to be otherwise—when I asked, I say, how it was possible for me to judge in this way, it was clear that I had found the unchangeable and true eternity of truth above my own changeable intelligence. Thus step by step was I led upwards, from bodies to the soul which perceives by means of the bodily senses, and thence to the soul's inward faculty, to which bodily sense reports external facts, and this belongs even to beasts, and thence again to the reasoning power, to whose judgment is referred the knowledge received by the bodily senses.

3. And when this power also within me found itself changeable, it lifted itself up to its own intelligence, and withdrew its thoughts from experience, abstracting itself from the contra-

---

[1] ἔτι ὀπισθοβαρὴς ὑπάρχων, Plotinus *Ennead* vi. 9, 4. The whole of this chapter is strongly Plotinian.

[2] Rom i. 20

dictory throng of sensuous images, that it might
find out what that light was wherein it was
bathed, when it cried out that beyond doubt the
unchangeable was better than the changeable,
and how it came to know the unchangeable,
which it must have known in some way or
another, for otherwise it could not have preferred
it so confidently to the changeable. And thus,
with the flash of one hurried glance, it attained
to the vision of THAT WHICH IS. And then at
last I saw Thy invisible things understood by
means of the things that are made,[1] but I could
not sustain my gaze; my weakness was dashed
back, and I was relegated to my ordinary experience, bearing with me nothing but a loving
remembrance, cherishing, as it were, the fragrance
of those viands which I was not yet able to
feed upon.

CHAPTER XVIII

Christ the only Way to Salvation.

SO I cast about for some way to attain a
strength that should be able to enjoy Thee;
nor could I find any, until I embraced the
mediator between God and man, the Man Christ
Jesus, who is over all, God blessed for ever,[2]
who calleth me and saith, "I am the Way, the
Truth, and the Life,"[3] who mingleth Himself

[1] Rom. i. 20. But the whole of this passage is
coloured by reminiscences of Plotinus.
[2] 1 Tim. ii. 5; Rom. ix. 5. [3] John xiv. 6.

with flesh, and is the food which I was as yet
unable to receive, because the Word was made
Flesh,[1] that Thy all-creative wisdom might
become milk for us babes. For as yet I did not
humbly hold the humble Lord Jesus, nor did I
know what His weakness was meant to teach us.
For Thy Word, the Eternal Truth, far exalted
above the higher parts of Thy creation, lifteth
up His subjects towards Himself, but in the
lower parts hath built for Himself a humble
dwelling of our clay, that so He might pull down
from themselves and win over to Himself those
whom He is to make subject, lowering their
pride and heightening their love, that they might
not stray farther afield in self-confidence, but
rather be made weak, seeing before their feet the
Godhead made weak by sharing our coats of
skins,[2] and that they might cast themselves
wearily upon It, and be uplifted by Its rising.

CHAPTER XIX

What he thought of the incarnation of Christ.

BUT I was otherwise minded, and thought of
my Lord Christ only as a man of excellent
wisdom, to whom none other could be compared.

[1] John i. 14.
[2] Origen thought that "the coats of skins" (Gen.
iii. 21) might signify the bodies in which Adam and
Eve were clothed on their expulsion from Paradise.

Especially because He was miraculously born of
a Virgin, to set us an example of despising
worldly things for the attainment of immortality,
and thus showed His divine care for us, I held
that He had merited the highest authority as a
teacher. But what sacramental meaning there
lay in "the Word was made Flesh" I could
not even guess. Only I knew from what scripture records about Him (that He ate, drank,
slept, walked, was joyful, was sorrowful, dis-
coursed) that the flesh was not united to Thy
Word without a human soul and mind. Every
one knows this who knows the unchangeableness
of Thy Word, which I knew by this time, as
far as I could, nor did I doubt it in any way.
For at one time to move the limbs by an act of
will, at another not, at one time to feel some
emotion, at another not, at one time to utter
intelligible sentences by verbal symbols, at another
not—these are the proper signs of a changeable
soul and mind. And if these were falsely attributed to Him by scripture, the truth of all scripture would come into jeopardy, nor would there
be left in scripture any faith to be the salvation
of the human race.

2. Therefore, because what is written is true,
I recognised the perfect man in Christ, not
merely the body of man, or the soul and the body
without the mind, but the soul and the mind

See *contra Celsum* iv. 40; *in Lev.* Hom. vi. 2. Ter-
tullian *de Res. Carnis* 7 rejects this allegorism. It
seems to have been derived from the Rabbis through
the Gnostics.

as well as the body, and this man I held to be
superior to all others, not because He was the
Person of Truth, but by some great excellence
and perfection of this human nature, due to the
participation of wisdom.   Alypius on the other
hand thought that the Catholics believed that
God was clothed in flesh in such a manner that,
besides the Godhead and the flesh, there was in
Christ, according to their teaching, neither the
soul nor the mind of man.   And on this account
he was drawn more slowly towards the true
Christian faith, because he felt convinced that
the acts recorded of Christ necessarily implied
a living and rational nature.   But afterwards he
discovered that this was in fact the error of the
Apollinarian heresy, and upon this he joyfully
submitted to the Catholic faith.   For myself, I
must confess, it was not till later that I learned
how the Catholic truth differs from the Photinian
untruth in the interpretation of the phrase " the
Word was made flesh."   Truly the refutation
of heretics brings into clearer relief the meaning
of Thy church, and the teaching of sound doctrine.   For there were also to be heresies, in
order that they which are approved may be made
manifest among the weak.[1]

[1] 1 Cor. xi. 19.

CHAPTER XX

The books of the Platonists deepen his understanding, but increase his pride.

BY the study of those Platonist books I was taught to seek for the incorporeal Truth, and beheld Thy invisible things understood by means of the things that are made; and, though cast back, I felt what the dulness of my soul did not permit me to gaze upon; I had no doubt that Thou art, and that Thou art infinite, though not diffused through space either finite or infinite; and that Thou truly art, because Thou art always the same, without any difference of parts or movement; and that everything else is derived from Thee, as is proved beyond possibility of denial by the very fact of its existence. Of all this I was convinced, yet was I too weak to enjoy Thee. I prated like one who knew, yet, unless I found Thy way in Christ our Saviour, what I deemed true was like to end in rue.[1] For I had begun to wish men to think me wise, drinking deep of that which was my punishment, and, when I should have wept, I was puffed up with knowledge.[2]

2. For where was that charity which buildeth up on the foundation of humility, which is Christ Jesus?[3] Or when would those books have

[1] *Non peritus sed periturus essem.*
[2] 1 Cor. viii. 1.   [3] 1 Cor. iii. 11; viii. 1.

taught me charity? It was, I do believe, Thy
will that I should plunge into them before I
studied Thy scripture, in order that I should
never forget what impression they made upon me,
and that, when afterwards I had been disciplined
by Thy books, and my wounds had been dressed
by Thy healing fingers, I should clearly and distinctly recognise the difference between presumption and confession, between those who see
the end of their journey but not the road by
which they travel, and those who see the road
leading to their blessed country, that country
which is no mere vision but a home. For, if I
had first been moulded by Thy Holy Writ, and
Thou hadst grown sweet to me in its companionship, and if afterwards I had lighted upon the
Platonic volumes, they might, perchance, have
torn me loose from the foundation of godliness,
or if I had persisted in the belief which I had
drawn from the wells of salvation, I might have
fancied that it could have been obtained from
Platonism alone.

CHAPTER XXI

*What he found in Holy Writ, and did not find in
Platonism.*

WITH most eager desire then did I fasten
upon the august writings of Thy Spirit,
and principally upon the Apostle Paul. I had

thought that he sometimes contradicted himself,
and that the drift of his teaching did not agree
with the testimony of the Law and the Prophets,
but now all these doubts fell dead. I saw that
those pure words had but one face, and I learned
to rejoice with trembling.[1] So I began; and I
found that whatever truth I had read in the Old
Testament was here combined with the exalta-
tion of Thy Grace. Hence he who sees must
not glory, as if he had not received,[2] not only
the thing that he sees, but the very power of
sight—for what is there that he has not received?
Hence he is not only exhorted to see, but
cleansed, that he may grasp Thee, who art ever
the same. Hence he, who cannot see afar off,
may yet enter upon the road that leads to attainment and seeing and grasping. For, though a
man delight in the law of God after the inner
man, what will he do with that other law in his
members, warring against the law of his mind,
and bringing him into captivity to the law of sin
which is in his members.[3] For Thou art
righteous, O Lord, but we have sinned and
committed iniquity, and done wickedly,[4] and Thy
hand has been heavy upon us, and we are justly
delivered over to that ancient sinner, the lord of
Death, because he persuaded our will to become
like unto his will, whereby he abode not in Thy
truth.

2. What shall wretched man do? Who shall

[1] Ps. ii. 11.   [2] 1 Cor. iv. 7.
[3] Rom. vii. 22-23.
[4] Dan. iii. 27-29 (Vulgate).

deliver him from the body of this death, except Thy Grace, through Jesus Christ our Lord,[1] whom Thou didst beget co-eternal with Thyself, and didst create in the beginning of Thy ways,[2] in whom the prince of this world found nothing worthy of death,[3] yet did he slay Him, and so the handwriting, which was contrary to us, was blotted out?[4] The books of the Platonists tell nothing of this. Those pages grave not the lineaments of this religion, the tears of confession, the troubled spirit, the broken and contrite heart, which are Thy sacrifice,[5] the salvation of the people, the Bride, the City, the earnest of the Holy Spirit, the Cup of our redemption. There no one sings, "Shall not my soul wait upon God, for of Him cometh my salvation. For He is my God and my salvation and my defence. I shall no more be moved."[6]

3. No one there hearkens to Him that calleth, "Come unto Me all ye that labour."[7] They think it scorn to learn from Him, because He is meek and lowly of heart. For Thou hast hidden these things from the wise and prudent, and hast revealed them unto babes.[8] It is one thing from some wooded height to behold the land of peace, yet find no road thereto, and struggle vainly towards it through pathless wilds, beset by the ambushments of runagates, with

---

[1] Rom. vii. 24, 25.   [2] Prov. viii. 22.
[3] John xiv. 30; Luke xxiii. 15.
[4] Col. ii. 14.   [5] Ps. li. 19.   [6] Ps. lxii. i. 2.
[7] Matt. xi. 28.   [8] Matt. xi. 25, 29.

their prince, the lion and the dragon,[1] it is another thing to march thitherwards along the high road, built by the care of the heavenly Emperor, whereon are no deserters from the heavenly army to rob the passer-by, for they shun it as a torment. These thoughts sank wondrously into my heart, when I read the least of Thy Apostles,[2] and had considered Thy works, and feared.

[1] Ps. xci. 13. [2] 1 Cor. xv. 9.

BOOK VIII

HE arrives at the most famous period of his life, his thirty-second year, in which he heard from Simplicianus the conversion of Victorinus and from Pontitianus the history of Antony; and, after a fierce struggle between the flesh and the spirit, cast his eyes upon the sacred volume of the Apostle in obedience to a voice from heaven; and, as he read, turned with his whole heart to the better way, and was entirely converted to God.

CHAPTER I

He determines to go to Simplicianus for advice.

O MY God, let me remember with thankfulness and confess Thy many mercies towards me. Let my bones be bathed in Thy love and say, "Lord who is like unto Thee,[1] Thou hast broken my bonds in sunder; I will offer unto Thee the sacrifice of thanksgiving." [2] How Thou didst break them I will declare, and all Thy worshippers, when they hear this, shall say, "Blessed be the Lord in heaven and on earth; great and wonderful is His Name." Thy words had stuck fast in my heart, and I was hedged round about on every side by Thee.[3] Of Thy eternal life I was certain, although I discerned it in a riddle, and, as it were, in a glass.[4] And I had been relieved of all doubt that there is an incorruptible substance, and that it is the source of every other substance, nor did I crave greater certainty about Thee, but greater steadfastness in Thee. And, as to my temporal life, all my plans were in confusion, and my heart still needed to be purged of the old leaven.[5] The Way, the Saviour Himself, pleased me

[1] Ps. xxxv. 10.　　[2] Ps. cxvi. 16.　　[3] Job i. 10.
[4] 1 Cor. xiii. 12.　　[5] 1 Cor. v. 7.

well, but as yet I was reluctant to pass through the strait gate.

2. And Thou didst put into my mind, and it seemed good in my sight, to go to Simplicianus, who appeared to me to be a good servant of Thine, and Thy grace shone forth in him. I had been told also that from his youth up he had lived in entire devotion to Thee. He was already aged, and, during the many years that he had spent in the good purpose of following Thy way, I thought he must have passed through much and learned much, and truly so he had. I resolved to speak with him of my agitations, hoping that out of his experience he would be able to tell me what was the right line of conduct for one who felt as I did about walking in the way. For I saw the church full; and one man was going this way and another that. But I could not be satisfied with the life I was living in the world; it was a heavy burden to me; and, now that my ambition no longer inflamed me as before with the hope of honour or wealth, my slavery was more than I could bear. For the old baits allured me no longer in comparison of Thy sweetness and the beauty of Thy house, which I loved.[1] But as yet I was tied fast by the love of a woman; nor did the Apostle forbid me to marry, although he counselled me to a better course, wishing earnestly that all men were even as himself.[2]

3. But I was weak, and chose the easier

[1] Ps. xxvi. 8.   [2] 1 Cor. vii. 7.

place, and for this single reason my whole life
was one of listless indecision, wasting away in
dull anxieties, because in many galling points
I was obliged to conform to the requirements
of married life, which bound me hand and
foot. I had heard from the mouth of Truth
that there are eunuchs who have made themselves eunuchs for the sake of the kingdom
of heaven : but (saith He) "whoso is able to
receive it, let him receive it."¹ Surely vain are
all men who have not the knowledge of God,
nor have been able from the good things that
are seen to find out Him that is.² But I lay no
longer in that vanity, I had climbed above it,
and, by the attesting voice of all creation, I had
found Thee our Creator, and Thy Word, God
with Thee, One God with Thee and the
Holy Spirit, by whom Thou didst create all
things.

4. There is also another sort of ungodly men,
who knowing God glorified Him not as God
neither were thankful.³ Into this also I had
fallen ; but Thy right hand, O God, held me
up,⁴ and called me away from that company,
and set me where I might recover. For Thou
hast said to man, " Behold the fear of the Lord
is wisdom ; " ⁵ and, " Be not wise in thine own
eyes," ⁶ because " they that professed themselves
to be wise became fools." ⁷ And I had already
found the goodly pearl ; I ought to have sold all

¹ Matt. xix. 12.   ² Wisdom xiii. 1.
³ Rom. i. 21.   ⁴ Ps. xviii. 35.   ⁵ Job xxviii. 28.
⁶ Prov. iii. 7.   ⁷ Rom. i. 22.

that I had and bought it,[1] and yet I could not make up my mind.

CHAPTER II

Simplicianus describes the conversion of the rhetorician Victorinus.

AND so I made my way to Simplicianus, the spiritual father of the then Bishop Ambrose, whom Ambrose truly loved as a father. To him I described all the mazes of my wanderings. But when I mentioned that I had read certain Platonic books translated into Latin by Victorinus,[2] rhetoric professor at Rome, who, as I had heard, had died a Christian, Simplicianus congratulated me on my good fortune in not having fallen in with the writings of other philosophers. They, he said, were full of fallacies and deceptions after the rudiments of this world,[3] whereas in the Platonists God and His Word were implied at every turn. Then, that he might encourage me to copy the humility of Christ, which is hidden from the wise and revealed to babes,[4] he spoke to me about Victorinus, whom he had known intimately at Rome. And I cannot refrain from repeating what he told me of him.

[1] Matt. xiii. 46.
[2] Victorinus Afer, see Canon Gore's article in the *Dictionary of Christian Biography.*
[3] Col. ii. 8.   [4] Matt. xi. 25.

2. For surely it is a glorious proof of Thy grace, which ought to be confessed unto Thee, when we consider how that old man, most learned, most skilled in all liberal sciences, who had read, criticised, explained so many works of philosophy, who had been the tutor of so many illustrious senators, who, for distinguished service in a high office, which the citizens of this world regard as eminent, had deserved and received a statue in the Roman Forum, who, up to advanced age, had been a worshipper of idols, a communicant of godless rites—rites which at that time swayed almost the whole of the Roman nobles, so much so that they inspired even into the populace the fear of that bestial crew, "barking Anubis and monstrous shapes of gods of every breed,"[1] which once had borne arms against Neptune and Venus and Minerva, which Rome, their conqueror, now adored, which old Victorinus had long championed with a voice of thunder—how, I say, that aged man did not blush to become the child of Thy Christ, the babe of Thy font, bowing his neck to the yoke of humility, and hardening his forehead against the reproach of the Cross.

3. O Lord, Lord, Who didst bow the heavens and come down, Who didst touch the mountains and they smoked,[2] how didst Thou wind Thy way into that breast? He used to read, as Simplicianus said, the Holy Scripture, and all Christian literature he studied and examined with great diligence. He used to say to Simplicianus,

[1] Virg. *Aen.* viii. 698.　　[2] Ps. cxliv. 5.

not in public but in the confidence of privacy, "You must know that I am already a Christian." To which Simplicianus replied, "I shall not believe it; nor shall I reckon you among Christians, till I see you in the Church of Christ." Victorinus laughed and rejoined, "So then walls make a Christian." Often he used to affirm that he was already a Christian, often Simplicianus made the same answer, often his jest about the walls was repeated. He was afraid to offend his friends, who were proud demon-worshippers, from the height of whose Babylonian dignity, as from the tops of cedars of Libanus which the Lord had not yet broken,[1] he fancied an avalanche of hostility would crash down upon him.

4. But by reading and reflection he gained strength; he feared to be denied by Christ before the holy angels, if he should fear to confess Him before men;[2] he saw that he would be guilty of a great crime, if he was ashamed of the sacraments of the humility of Thy Word, and not ashamed of the godless worship of those proud demons, whereof he had been a proud follower and participant; he was disgusted with vanity and blushed for the Truth; and so, quite suddenly and unexpectedly, he said to Simplicianus, as Simplicianus told me, "Let us go to church; I want to become a Christian." Simplicianus went with him, scarce able to contain himself for joy. He received the first sacraments of instruction, and not long afterwards gave in

[1] Ps. xxix. 5.   [2] Luke ix. 26.

his name, that he might receive the baptism of regeneration, to the great wonder of Rome and the great joy of the Church. The proud saw and were wroth; they gnashed with their teeth and melted away.[1] But the Lord God was the hope of His servant, and he regarded not vanities and lying madness.[2]

5. Finally, when the hour arrived for making the public profession of faith, which at Rome is made by those who are about to enter into Thy grace from a platform, in full sight of the faithful people, in a set form of words repeated by heart, the presbyters, Simplicianus said, would have given Victorinus leave to make his profession in private, this being not unusual in the case of persons who had reason for shrinking from so trying an ordeal, but he deliberately chose to profess his salvation in the sight of the holy congregation. For there was no salvation in the rhetoric which he had taught; yet he had professed that openly. Why then should he shrink from naming Thy Word before the sheep of Thy flock, when he had not shrunk from uttering his own words before troops of madmen?

6. And so, when he mounted the platform to deliver his profession, all who knew him uttered his name with a cry of delight. And who was there that knew him not? And so a whisper was heard running all round that jubilant assembly, "Victorinus! Victorinus!" Sudden was the sound of exultation, when they saw him; sudden was the hush of attention, that they might hear.

[1] Ps. cxii. 10.   [2] Ps. xl. 5.

He repeated the true faith with unfaltering confidence, and all would have clasped him to their hearts, yea, they did clasp him to their hearts with the arms of love and joy.

CHAPTER III

Why God and his Angels rejoice more over the Conversion of Sinners.

O GOOD God, why is it that men feel higher joy over the salvation of a soul despaired of, or rescued from more deadly peril, than over one which has never lost hope, or never been in such imminent danger? Because Thou also, O merciful Father, rejoicest more over one that repenteth, than over ninety and nine just persons that need no repentance. So we also listen with great delight, when we hear how the wandering sheep is carried back on the shepherd's shoulders amid the joy of the angels, or how, when the piece of money is restored to its home in the treasury, the neighbours rejoice with the woman who hath found it. And the joy of the festival of Thy house draws tears from our eyes, when in Thy house we read the story of that younger son, who was dead and is alive again, was lost and is found.[1] For of a truth it is Thou that dost rejoice in us and in Thy angels, who are holy through holy charity.

[1] Luke xv., *passim.*

For Thou art for ever the same, because Thou knowest unchangeably all things, which are not for ever nor unchangeable. Why then does our soul delight more at finding or regaining the things that it loves than in their constant possession? For everything bears witness, everything is full of voices that cry " So it is."

2. The general triumphs in his victory, and there would have been no victory had there been no battle; and the more desperate the battle, the greater is the joy of the triumph. The tempest tosses the mariners, menacing shipwreck; every cheek grows pale in presence of death. The sky clears, the sea is calmed, and their exultation is as high, as their fears were deep. A dear one is sick; his pulse foretells the worst; all who long for his recovery are sick at heart from sympathy. There comes a favourable turn, but the invalid cannot yet walk with his old strength, and straightway there is such a jubilation as there never was while he was well and walked firmly.

3. Even the pleasures of life men acquire, and acquire by pain, pain which is not sudden and involuntary, but deliberately incurred. There is no pleasure in eating or drinking, unless there is first the pain of hunger and thirst. Hard drinkers will eat salt viands in order to create a painful fever; this the draught allays, and so pleasure is gained. And it is the regular custom that the bride is not bestowed in marriage immediately upon betrothal, lest the husband should scorn the gift which he did not sigh for through a long engagement. It is so with base and accursed

pleasures; it is so with permitted and lawful pleasures; it is so even with the purest and loveliest friendship; it is so with him who was dead and is alive again, was lost and is found. Everywhere the greater joy follows upon a greater pain.

4. What means this, O Lord my God, since Thou art Thine own eternal joy, and there are some creatures about Thee who ever rejoice in Thee? Why is it that, in our part of creation, there is this alternation of need and satisfaction, quarrels and love? Is it our law? Didst Thou give us so much and no more, when from the height of heaven to the depth of earth, from the beginning to the end of time, from the angel to the worm, from the first movement to the last, Thou wast assigning their proper place, their proper season to every kind of thing that is good, to all Thy righteous works? Alas! how high art Thou in the height, how deep in the depth! Thou never leavest us, yet how hard is it to return to Thee! Come, Lord, and work; arouse us and incite; kindle us, sweep us onwards; be fragrant as flowers, sweet as honey; teach us to love and to run.

CHAPTER IV

Why we ought to rejoice more over the conversion of famous men.

A RE there not many who, out of a deeper pit of darkness than Victorinus, return to Thee, draw near to Thee, receive the illumination of that Light, which, whoso receiveth, receives from Thee power to become Thy son?[1] Yet if they are less known to the people, even those who know them rejoice for them less. For, when joy is shared with many, the joy of each is richer, because they warm one another, catch fire from one another. Again, because they are known to many, they influence many towards salvation, and lead the way which many will follow. Therefore, even they who took the way before them, rejoice over them greatly, because they do not rejoice over them alone. For far be it from us, that in Thy tabernacle the persons of the rich should be accepted before the poor, or the noble before the lowly, seeing that Thou hast chosen the weak things of the world to confound the strong; and the base things of this world and things despised hast Thou chosen, and things which are not, that Thou mightest bring to nought things that are.[2]

2. And yet even that least of Thy Apostles by whose tongue Thou didst utter these words—

[1] John i. 9, 12. [2] 1 Cor. i. 27, 28.

when Paulus, the proconsul, his pride being
broken by the preacher's sword, bowed beneath
.he easy yoke of Thy Christ, and became an
officer of the Great King—even he chose to be
called Paul instead of Saul, to commemorate that
glorious victory. For the Enemy is more utterly
beaten in one of whom he has more hold, and
through whom he has hold of more. And he
has more hold of the proud by means of their
rank, and through them he has hold of more by
means of their influence. The more, therefore,
the world prized the heart of Victorinus, which
the devil held as an impregnable stronghold, and
the tongue of Victorinus, that sharp strong weapon
with which the devil had slain so many, the more
exultingly must Thy children rejoice, because our
King was binding the strong man,[1] and they saw
his vessels taken from him and cleansed, and
made fit for Thy honour, and serviceable to the
Lord for every good work.[2]

CHAPTER V

What difficulties retarded the conversion of
Augustine.

BUT, when Thy man Simplicianus related to
me this history of Victorinus, I was eager
to imitate him. This was the effect that he
desired to produce. But when he went on to
tell how, in the reign of the Emperor Julian,

[1] Matt. xii. 29.   [2] 2 Tim. ii. 21.

Christians were prohibited by an express law from teaching literature and rhetoric, and how Victorinus, in ready obedience to the law, chose to abandon his wordy school rather than Thy Word, with which Thou makest eloquent the tongues of babes,[1] I counted him not so much brave as happy, because he found a reason for giving his time wholly to Thee. For this was what I was panting to do; but as yet I was bound by the iron chain of my own will. The enemy held fast my will, and had made of it a chain, and bound me tight therewith. For from a perverse will came lust, and the service of lust ended in habit, and acquiescence in habit produced necessity. These were the links of what I call my chain, and they held me bound in hard slavery. But the new will which had sprung up in me, the will to serve Thee for nought and to enjoy Thee, O God, the one certain joy, was not yet strong enough to master the old time-hardened will. So my two wills, the old and the new, the carnal and the spiritual, were in conflict, and their discord paralysed my soul.

2. Thus I came to understand by my own experience what I had read of the flesh lusting against the spirit and the spirit against the flesh.[2] My self was in both; but my true self was in that which I approved in myself, not in that which I disapproved. For in the latter it was now not really I that was concerned, because here I was rather an unwilling sufferer than a willing actor. And yet I had myself armed

[1] Wisdom x. 21.   [2] Gal. v. 17.

habit against myself, for I had willingly come to be what I unwillingly found myself. And who can justly complain when just punishment falls upon the sinner? No longer could I plead the excuse with which I was wont to blind myself, that I could not as yet cast the world aside and serve Thee, because I did not clearly perceive the truth; for by this time I did clearly perceive it. But I was still bound to earth, and refused to enlist under Thy banner; and I was as much afraid of leaving my baggage behind as I ought to have been afraid of cumbering myself with it. So the heavy burden of the world seemed delightful, as in a dream, and my musings on Thee were like the struggles of one who would awake, but falls back overcome by depths of slumber. And as no one wishes to sleep for ever, for all men rightly count waking better, and yet a man will not break his slumber when his limbs are heavy with drowsiness, and is glad to sleep on, though his reason disapproves and the hour for rising has struck, so I knew for certain that it was better to yield to Thy love than to my lust, but the love charmed and could not prevail, the lust pleased and bound me.

3. For I could not answer Thee when Thou saidst: "Awake thou that sleepest, and arise from the dead, and Christ shall give thee light." [1] On all sides Thou didst show me that Thy words are true, and the truth confounded me, so that I could make no reply but slow and drowsy words: "Presently, O presently; let me be a little

[1] Eph. v. 14.

while." But my "presently, presently," had no present, and the little while proved a long while. Vainly did I delight in Thy law after the inward man, while another law in my members was warring against the law of my mind, and bringing me into captivity to the law of sin, which was in my members.[1] For the law of sin is the tyranny of habit, by which the mind is dragged and gripped against its will, yet deservedly, because it formed the habit willingly. Wretched man that I was; who could deliver me from the body of this Death? who but Thy grace through Jesus Christ our Lord?

CHAPTER VI

Pontitianus describes the life of Antony, the Egyptian Monk.

AND now will I tell and confess unto Thy Name, O Lord my Helper and my Redeemer,[2] how Thou didst deliver me from the bond of the sexual desire by which I was so tightly held, and from the slavery of worldly affairs. I was pursuing my usual life, with ever-growing dissatisfaction, and daily was I sighing unto Thee. I attended Thy church, whenever there was a pause in that business under the burden whereof I groaned. With me was Alypius, now released from his legal duties after

[1] Rom. vii. 23, 25. [2] Ps. xix. 14.

a third term of office as assessor, waiting to sell his experience to a new purchaser, as I was selling such faculty of speech as could be imparted by a teacher. Nebridius had proved his affection for us by accepting the post of lecturer under Verecundus, a citizen of Milan, professor of grammar, and one of our closest allies, who was in great need of a loyal colleague, and called, with the right of friendship, for the services of one of our company.

2. It was no desire of advancement, therefore, that had attracted Nebridius, for he might have obtained higher remuneration if he had chosen to keep to the teaching of literature, but he was too sweet and gentle a friend to refuse a request which appealed to his love. Yet he bore himself most discreetly, shunning the acquaintance of the great ones of this world, lest it should unsettle his mind; he wished to keep his freedom, and reserve as many hours as possible of leisure for thought, or reading, or hearing lectures on philosophy.

3. On a certain day, then, when Nebridius for some reason was not present, it happened that Pontitianus paid a visit to Alypius and myself at our house. He was an African, and so a fellow-countryman, and held high rank in the household. He had some request to make, and we sat down and conversed. He noticed a volume lying on the draught table before us, picked it up, opened it, and to his great surprise found that it was the Apostle Paul, for what he expected to see was one of my wearisome rhetorical

manuals. He looked at me with a smile, and told me how delighted he was to find so unpectedly that book, and that alone on my table. For he was a faithful Christian, and often prostrated himself before Thee, our God, in church in long and frequent prayer. I replied that I spent much time over the scriptures, and this led him on to speak of Antony, the Egyptian monk, whose name was held in high honour by Thy servants, though I had never heard it till that hour. When he discovered my ignorance he enlarged his discourse, marvelling at our ignorance of so great a man, and gently showing us how great he was.

4. We listened with amazement to the tale of Thy wonders, so freshly wrought, almost in our own lifetime, so well attested, springing from the true faith and the bosom of the Catholic Church. We were all alike surprised, Alypius and I because the history was so extraordinary; he because we had never heard it. Thence he passed to speak of the crowded monasteries, and the ways of Thy sweetness, and the teeming solitudes of the desert, all strange news to us. There was a monastery at Milan, outside the city walls, full of good brothers, of whom Ambrose was foster-father; yet we had never heard of it. He went on talking, and we listened in silence. So he was led to tell us how once he and three of his comrades at Treves—the Emperor being detained at the afternoon games in the circus—went out for a stroll in the gardens beneath the city walls; how they parted company, two going off

s

by themselves; how these two entered aimlessly into a house wherein dwelt certain of Thy servants, men poor in spirit, of whom is the kingdom of heaven,[1] and found there a volume containing the life of Antony.

5. One of them began to read, and as he read his soul caught fire, so that then and there he began to think of plunging into the monastic life, and exchanging his worldly service for Thine. He was one of the officials of the Ministry of the Interior.[2] Suddenly he was filled with holy love and sober shame, and, as if angered with himself, fixed his eyes upon his friend, saying, " Tell me, prithee, what goal are we seeking in all these toils of ours? What is it that we desire? What do we look to gain in the service? Can we hope in the palace to attain anything better than the friendship of the Emperor? How frail, how beset with perils is that prize! Through what dangers must we climb to a greater danger! And when shall we succeed? But, if I choose, I can be the friend of God from this moment."

6. He spoke, and, torn by the pangs of the new birth, returned to the book. As he read he was changed in the inner man, which Thou canst see, and his mind was alienated from the world, as soon appeared. For he read, with heart like a stormy sea; more than once he groaned, but he saw the better course, and made up his resolve. And so at last he said quite calmly to his friend, " I have broken with ambition, and determined

[1] Matt. v. 3.
[2] *Agentes in Rebus.* See Facciolati, *Agens.*

to serve God. I am going to begin this moment, and here. If you do not care to follow my example, do not oppose me." "The service," replied the other, "is noble, and the wage is great; I will be your brother in arms." So both became Thine, and "built a tower at their own cost," having determined to give up all and follow Thee.[1] Shortly afterwards Pontitianus and his companions, who had been walking in a different part of the garden and looking for the lost couple, arrived at the house, where they found them, and pressed them to return, as the sun had already set. But the two friends told them of the resolve which had so wonderfully sprung up and taken shape in their minds, and begged them not to take it ill if they refused to go with them. "So we," said Pontitianus, "who could not change our course, shed tears, not for them but for ourselves; we congratulated them on their godly decision, commended ourselves to their prayers, and went back to the palace, dragging our hearts along the ground, while they remained in the house, with hearts uplifted to heaven." Both these men were betrothed, but their wives, that should have been, followed the example of their lovers, and consecrated their virginity to Thee

[1] Luke xiv. 28, 33.

CHAPTER VII.

*How the narrative of Pontitianus pricked
Augustine to the heart.*

SUCH was the story that Pontitianus told.
But, whilst he was speaking, Thou, O
Lord, didst turn me round into my own sight.
I had set myself, as it were, upon my own back,
because I was unwilling to see myself, and now
Thou didst place me before my own eyes so that
I beheld how ugly I was, how deformed, and
filthy, and spotted, and ulcerous. I beheld and
shuddered, yet whither could I flee from myself?
And, if I strove not to look upon myself, the
tale of Pontitianus caught me again, and again
didst Thou hold up to me my own portrait, and
forced my eyes to gaze upon my very features, so
that I might discover and loathe my own iniquity.[1] I knew it; but feigned ignorance, and
winked at it, and forgot it. But at that moment
the warmer my love for that pair of friends,
whose wholesome resolve to give themselves up
altogether into Thy healing hands was still ringing in my ears, the deeper was my hatred of
myself. How many of my years—perhaps twelve
whole years—had run to waste since the day
when, as a youth of nineteen, I had read the
Hortensius of Cicero, and heard the call to the
study of wisdom. My plain duty was to scorn

[1] Ps. xxxvi. 2.

earthly delights and devote myself to the search after that happiness whereof the mere pursuit— not to speak of its attainment—is better than the possession of all the treasures and kingdoms of the world, better than all bodily pleasures, though they were to be had for a word. And yet I was wasting time.

2. Yea, wretched, O wretched youth that I had been, on the very threshold of my youth, I had even begged of Thee the gift of chastity; but I had said "Give me chastity and self-control, but not just yet." For I was afraid lest Thou shouldest hear me in a moment, and in a moment heal that disease of lust, which I wanted to be sated, not eradicated. And I had wandered along the evil ways of godless superstition, not that I thought them right, only because I preferred them to others, which I angrily denounced without any serious reflection. And I flattered myself that the reason why, from day to day, I hesitated to cast off the world and its hopes and follow Thee alone, was that I could find no certain goal. And now the day had come when I was laid bare in my own sight, and the stern voice of conscience demanded "Where is thy tongue? Wast thou not wont to say that thou wouldest not cast off the pack of thy vanity for an uncertain truth. Lo, the truth is certain, and thou art still bending under thy pack, while others, who have not wearied themselves in research, nor spent a long ten years in study, are putting forth wings from free shoulders."

3. Thus did a horrible shame gnaw and confound my soul while Pontitianus was speaking. He ended his tale, despatched the business which had brought him to our house, and departed. But how did I reproach myself! with what sharp reasons did I flog my soul to make it follow me in my effort to follow Thee. And it would not; it refused and would not even make an excuse. All its arguments had been tried and found wanting, yet it resisted in sullen disquiet, fearing, as if it were death, the closing of that running sore of evil habit by which it was being wasted to death.

CHAPTER VIII

He goes into the garden. What befell him there.

DISORDERED in look and mind by this desperate wrestle with my own soul in the secret chambers of my own heart, I fell upon Alypius crying out, "What has come to us? What means this tale that thou hast heard? Simple men arise and take heaven by violence,[1] and we with all our heartless learning—see how we are wallowing in flesh and blood. Shall we stand still because they have taken the lead? Shall we not follow if we could not lead?" I scarcely knew what I said, and flung away, leaving him staring in silent astonishment. For

[1] Matt. xi. 12.

my voice was changed; my face, eyes, colour,
tone expressed my meaning more clearly than
my words.

2. There was a garden to our lodging, of
which we were free, as indeed we were of the
whole house. For our host, the master of the
house, did not live there. Thither the tumult
of my breast drove me, where no one could
interrupt the duel into which I had entered with
myself, until it should reach the issue which Thou
alone couldest foresee. I was mad, unto salvation; I was dying, unto life; I knew what evil
thing I was; what good thing I was soon to be
I knew not. I fled then into the garden, and
Alypius followed me step for step. For I had
no secret wherein he did not share, and how
could he leave me in such distress? We sat
down, as far from the house as possible. I was
groaning in spirit, shaken with a gust of indignation, because I could not enter into Thy
Will and Covenant, O my God; yet all my
bones were crying out that this was the way,
the best of all ways, and no ship is needed for
that way, nor chariot, no, nor feet, for it is not
so far as from the house to the spot where we
were seated.

3. For to go along that road, aye, and to
reach the goal, is all one with the will to go;
but it must be a strong and single will, not a
broken-winged wish fluttering hither and thither,
rising with one pinion, struggling and falling with
the other. In fine, in the midst of that passionate
indecision, I was doing many things which men

sometimes will, yet cannot perform, because they
have lost a limb, because their limbs are bound
with fetters, or enfeebled by disease, or incapaci-
tated in some other way. If I tore my hair, or
beat my brow, or clasped my hands about my
knees, it was because I willed to do so. Yet I
might have willed in vain, if the nerves had not
obeyed my bidding. Many things then I did,
in which will and power to do were not the
same, yet did not that one thing which seemed
to me infinitely more desirable, which, before
long, I should have power to will, because,
before long, I should certainly will to will it.
For in this the power of willing is the power of
doing, and yet I could not do it. And so my
body lent a ready obedience to the slightest
desire of the soul, moving its limbs in instant
compliance, while my soul could not aid itself in
carrying out its great resolve, which needed but
resolve to accomplish it.

CHAPTER IX

*Why the mind is not obeyed when it commands
itself.*

NOW whence and why is this strange anomaly?
Let Thy mercy shine as the light; and
suffer me to ask, if perchance I may find an
answer amid the dark places of human chastisement, and the midnight of the contrition of the

sons of Adam. Whence is this anomaly and why? Mind commands body, and there is instant obedience; mind commands mind, and there is rebellion. Mind commands the hand to move, and so facile is the process that you can hardly distinguish the order from its fulfilment; now the mind is mind and the hand is body. Mind commands mind to will, and, though it is one, it will not hear. Whence and why is this anomaly? I say it commands to will; and it would not command unless it did will, and yet its command is inoperative.

2. But it does not will wholly, and therefore it does not command wholly. For it commands, in so far as it wills, and its command is not executed, in so far as it does not will. For the will commands that there should be a will, and not another will but itself. Certainly it is not the full will that commands, hence it is not the very thing that it commands. For if it were the full will, it would not even command itself to be, because it would be already. And so this " will and will not" is no anomaly, but a sickness of the mind, which is weighed down by evil habit, and cannot rise wholly when uplifted by truth. And so there are two wills, because one of them is not whole, and one of them possesses what the other lacks.

CHAPTER X

Against the Manicheans who because there are two contrary wills affirm the existence of two contrary natures.

LET them perish from Thy presence,[1] O God, yea, and they do perish, those vain talkers and seducers of the soul,[2] who, because they have observed that in the act of deliberation there are two wills, maintain that there are two minds of differing natures, the one good and the other bad. They themselves are bad, while they hold these bad ideas, yet will they become good, if they see the truth and assent unto the truth, that Thy Apostle may say to them, "Ye were sometimes darkness, but now are ye light in the Lord." [3] For these Manichees, wishing to be light not in the Lord but in themselves, imagining the essence of the soul to be the essence of God, have become thicker darkness than they were, for in their dread arrogance they have gone farther away from Thee, from Thee, the true Light which lighteth every man that cometh into the world.[4] Mark what you say, and blush for shame. Draw near unto Him and be lightened, and your faces shall not be ashamed.[5] Who was it that willed, who was it that could not will, when I was deliberating whether I should not at once serve

[1] Ps. lxviii. 2.   [2] Titus i. 10.   [3] Eph. v. 8.
[4] John i. 9.   [5] Ps. xxxiv. 5.

the Lord my God, as I had long purposed to do? Was it not I, I myself? I could not fully will, I could not fully will not. And so I was at war with myself, and dragged asunder by myself. And the strife was against my will, yet it showed not the presence of a second mind, but the punishment of the one I had. Therefore it was no more I that wrought it, but sin that dwelt in me,[1] the punishment of a sin that was more voluntary, because I was a son of Adam. For, if there are as many opposing natures as opposing wills, there will be not two but many more.

2. If a man deliberates whether he shall go to their conventicle or to the theatre they cry, " See, he has two natures; the good one draws him to us, the evil drags him back. For how else shall we account for this halting between conflicting wills?" But I say that both wills are bad, that which draws him to them, not less than that which drags him back to the theatre. They naturally think it a good will which pulls in their direction. But suppose one of our people is tossed about between two wills, to go to the theatre or to go to our church—will they not be puzzled what to say? Either they must reluctantly confess that the will which carries a man to our church is as good as that which carries their own professors and adherents to theirs, or they must allow that two evil natures and two evil minds are fighting in one man, and in this case their favourite doctrine that one is good and the other evil falls to the ground, or they must

[1] Rom. vii. 17.

be converted to the truth, and cease to deny that, when a man deliberates, one soul is agitated by opposing wills. Let them then no longer maintain that, when two wills are contending in one man, two antagonistic minds, one good and one evil, are struggling over two antagonistic substances, created by two antagonistic principles.

3. For Thou, O God of truth, dost reprove and confute and convict them, for both wills may be bad, as when a man deliberates whether he shall murder by poison or by knife; whether he shall seize upon this field or the other, supposing that he cannot get both; whether he shall purchase pleasure by wantonness, or keep his money through covetousness; whether he shall go to the theatre or the circus, if there are shows at both on the same day; and there may be a third course open to him, for there may be a chance of robbing a house, and even a fourth, for there may be an opportunity of committing adultery as well.

4. Suppose that all these objects present themselves at the same time, and are all equally desired, yet cannot all be secured together, in this case they rend the mind with four conflicting wills, or even more, if there are more objects of desire. Yet they would not say that all these are different substances. The case is the same with good wills. For I ask them whether it is good to find sober delight in reading the Apostle, or in a psalm, or in discoursing upon the Gospel. They will say that each is good. What then if all are equally delightful, and all at the same time?

Are not different wills distracting the heart, when we consider which we shall prefer? All are good, but they are in conflict, till one is chosen, and the will is no longer divided between many objects but poured in its full strength upon that one. So also, when eternity attracts us from above and the pleasure of earthly goods pulls us down from below, the soul does not will either the one or the other with all its force, but it is the same soul; and the reason why it is so vexed and torn is that truth forces it to love the better, while custom will not suffer it to cast away the worse.

CHAPTER XI

The flesh wrestles with the spirit in Augustine.

THUS was I sick and tormented, reproaching myself more bitterly than ever, rolling and writhing in my chain till it should be wholly broken, for at present, though all but snapped, it still held me fast. And Thou, O Lord, wast urgent in my inmost heart, plying with austere mercy the scourges of fear and shame, lest I should fail once more, and the remnant of my worn and slender fetter, instead of breaking, should grow strong again, and bind me harder than ever. For I kept saying within myself, "O let it be now, let it be now;" and as I spoke the word I was on the verge of resolution. I was on the point of action, yet acted not; still

I did not slip back into my former indifference,
but stood close and took fresh breath. I tried
again, and came a little nearer and a little nearer,
I could all but touch and reach the goal, yet I
did not quite reach or touch it, because I still
shrank from dying unto death and living unto
life, and the worse, which was ingrained, was
stronger in me than the better, which was un-
trained. And the moment, which was to make
me different, affrighted me more the nearer it
drew, but it no longer repelled or daunted, it
only chilled me.

2. Trifles of trifles and vanities of vanities,
my old mistresses, held me back; they caught
hold of the garment of my flesh and whispered
in my ear, "Can you let us go? and from that
instant we shall see you no more for ever; and
from that instant this and that will be forbidden
you for ever." What did they mean, O my
God, what did they mean by "this and that?"
O let Thy mercy guard the soul of Thy servant
from the vileness, the shame that they meant!
As I heard them, they seemed to have shrunk
to half their former size. No longer did they
meet me face to face with open contradiction,
but muttered behind my back, and, when I
moved away, plucked stealthily at my coat to
make me look back. Yet, such was my indecision, that they prevented me from breaking
loose, and shaking myself free, and running after
the voice that called me away; for strong habit
supported them, asking me, "Do you think you
san live without them."

3. But the voice of Habit had lost its persuasion. For in that quarter to which I had set my face and was fain to fly, there dawned upon me the chaste dignity of Continence, calm and cheerful but not wanton, modestly alluring me to come and doubt not, holding out to welcome and embrace me her pious hands full of good examples. There might I see boys and girls, a goodly array of youth and of every age, grave widows and aged virgins, and in every one of them all was Continence herself, not barren but a fruitful mother of children,[1] of joys born of Thee, her husband, O Lord. And she smiled upon me with a challenging smile, as if she would say, " Canst not thou do what these have done ? Was it their power, was it not that of the Lord their God, that gave them strength ? The Lord their God gave me unto them. Thou standest on thyself, and therefore standest not. Cast thyself on Him ; fear not ; He will not flinch, and thou wilt not fall. Cast thyself boldly upon Him ; He will sustain thee, and heal thee." And I blushed, for still I heard the whispers of the daughters of vanity, and still I hung in the wind. And again she seemed to say, " Stop thine ears against thy unclean members upon earth, that they may be mortified. They tell thee of delights, but not according to the law of the Lord thy God." [2] Such was the debate that raged in my heart, myself battling against

[1] Ps. cxiii. 8.

[2] Ps. cxix. 85, agreeing with Ps. cxviii. 85 of the Vulgate.

myself. Alypius kept close to my side and waited in silence to see the issue of my strange agitation.

CHAPTER XII

How by a voice and by the words of the Apostle he was wholly converted.

NOW, when deep reflection brought forth from its secret stores the whole cloud of my misery, and piled it up in the sight of my heart, there rose a whirlwind, carrying with it a violent burst of tears. And hereupon I rose and left Alypius, till my weeping and crying should be spent. For solitude seemed fitter for tears. So I went farther off, till I could feel that even his presence was no restraint upon me. Thus it was with me, and he guessed my feelings. I suppose I had said something before I started up; and he noticed that my voice was fraught with tears. So he remained upon the bench lost in wonder. I flung myself down under a figtree, and gave my tears free course, and the floods of mine eyes broke forth, an acceptable sacrifice in Thy sight.[1] And I cried unto Thee incessantly, not in these words, but to this purpose, "And Thou, O Lord, how long? How long, O Lord; wilt Thou be angry for ever? O remember not our iniquities of old times."[2] For

[1] Ps. li. 19.   [2] Ps. lxxix. 5, 8.

I felt that I was held fast by them, and I went on wailing, "How long, how long? to-morrow and to-morrow? Why not now? why not this hour make an end of my vileness?"

2. Thus I spoke, weeping in bitter contrition of heart, when, lo, I heard a voice from the neighbouring house. It seemed as if some boy or girl, I knew not which, was repeating in a kind of chant the words, "Take and read, take and read." Immediately, with changed countenance, I began to think intently whether there was any kind of game in which children sang those words; but I could not recollect that I had ever heard them. I stemmed the rush of tears, and rose to my feet; for I could not think but that it was a divine command to open the Bible, and read the first passage I lighted upon. For I had heard that Antony had happened to enter a church at the moment when this verse of the Gospel was being read, "Go, sell all that thou hast and give to the poor, and thou shalt have treasure in heaven; and come and follow Me," [1] that he had taken these words home to himself, and by this oracle been converted to Thee on the spot.

3. I ran back then to the place where Alypius was sitting; for, when I quitted him, I had left the volume of the Apostle lying there. I caught it up, opened it, and read in silence the passage on which my eyes first fell, "Not in rioting and drunkenness, not in chambering and wantonness, not in strife and envying: but put ye on the

[1] Matt. xix. 21.

T

Lord Jesus Christ, and make not provision for the flesh to fulfil the lusts thereof." [1] No further would I read, nor was it necessary. As I reached the end of the sentence, the light of peace seemed to be shed upon my heart, and every shadow of doubt melted away. I put my finger, or some other mark, between the leaves, closed the volume, and with calm countenance told Alypius. And then he revealed to me his own feelings, which were unknown to me. He asked to see what I had read. I shewed him the text, and he read a little further than I had done, for I knew not what followed. What followed was this: "Him that is weak in the faith receive." [2] This he explained to me as applying to himself. These words of warning gave him strength, and with good purpose and resolve, following the bent of his moral character, which had always been much better than mine, without any painful hesitation, he cast in his lot with me. Immediately we went in to my mother, and to her great joy told her what had happened. But, when we explained to her how it had come to pass, she was filled with exultation and triumph, and blessed Thee, who art able to do above that we ask or think. [3] For she saw that Thou hadst granted her far more than she had ever asked for me in all her tearful lamentations. For so completely didst Thou convert me to Thyself that I desired neither wife nor any hope of this world, but set my feet on the rule of faith, as she had

[1] Rom. xiii. 13, 14.   [2] Rom. xiv. 1.
[3] Eph. iii. 20.

seen me in her vision so many years ago.   So
Thou didst turn her mourning into joy,[1] joy
fuller by far than she had ventured to pray for,
dearer and purer by far than that which she had
hoped to find in the children of my flesh.

[1] Ps. xxx. 11.

BOOK IX

He tells how he determined to resign
his Rhetoric Professorship, but
deferred his resignation to the
time of the vintage holidays,
which were close at hand. Then
he tells of his retirement to the
country house of his friend Verecundus, of his Baptism, and of
the virtues and the death of his
mother Monnica ; this happened
after his Baptism in the same year,
the thirty-third year of Augustine's age.

CHAPTER I.

He praises the goodness of God, and acknowledges his own misery.

O LORD, I am Thy servant; I am Thy servant and the son of Thine handmaid. Thou hast burst my bonds in sunder; to Thee will I offer the sacrifice of praise.[1] Let my heart and my tongue praise Thee, and let all my bones say, "O Lord, who is like unto Thee?"[2] Let them speak, and do Thou answer, and say unto my soul, "I am thy salvation."[3] Who am I, and what am I? What evil is there not in me and my deeds? or if not in my deeds, in my words! or if not in my words, in my will? But Thou, O Lord, art good and merciful. Thy right hand had respect unto the abyss of my death, and from the bottom of my heart did drain dry that sea of corruption. And what was that corruption, but that what Thou willest I willed not, and what Thou willest not I willed.

2. Yet where was my free will all through those years, and from what hidden recess was it called forth in a moment, so that I could put my neck under Thy easy yoke and my shoulders

[1] Ps. cxvi. 17, 18.   [2] Ps. xxxv. 10.
[3] Ps. xxxv. 3.

295

under Thy light burden,[1] O Christ Jesus, my Helper and my Redeemer?[2] How sweet did it seem to me in a moment to taste no more the sweetness of folly; it was joy to cast away what I had feared to lose. For Thou didst cast it out, Thou true and sovereign sweetness. Thou didst cast it out and fill its place, Thou who art sweeter than any pleasure, though not to flesh and blood; brighter than any light, though hidden behind the inmost veil; exalted above all honour, though not to them that are exalted in their own eyes. Henceforth my soul was delivered from the gnawing anxieties of ambition and gain, from wallowing in the mud and scratching the swinish itch of lust; and I prattled like a child to Thee, O Lord my God, my Light, my Wealth, my Salvation.

CHAPTER II.

He puts off the resignation of his Rhetoric Professorship till the Vintage Holidays.

AND I determined, as in Thy sight, to withdraw the service of my tongue, not with passionate abruptness, but by gentle degrees, from the market of verbosity; so that those boys who studied, not Thy law, not Thy peace, but lying frenzy and forensic war, should no longer buy from my lips the weapons for their madness. Fortunately but very few days remained before

[1] Matt. xi. 30.   [2] Ps. xix. 14.

the vintage and the holidays, and I resolved to make the best of them, so that I might resign in due form, for I could not put myself up to sale again, now that I had been bought by Thee. My plan then was known to Thee ; to men, save to my own friends, it was not known.   For we had agreed that it should not be made public ; though, as we climbed up from the valley of tears and sang the song of Degrees,[1] Thou hadst given us sharp arrows and hot burning coals to stop that deceitful tongue, which opposes under the guise of advice, and devours what it loves as though it were food.   Thou hadst pierced our hearts with the arrows of Thy love, and Thy words stuck fast in our flesh, and the examples of Thy servants, whom Thou hadst changed from black to shining white and from death to life, heaped themselves up in the bosom of our reflection, and burned up all our sluggish irresolution, so that we could not fall into the pit again ; yes, they kindled in us so strong a flame, that every breath of contradiction from the deceitful tongue served only to fan the fire.

2. Nevertheless, seeing that for the sake of Thy name, which Thou hast hallowed through all the world, our vow and purpose would certainly find some also who would praise it, we thought it would seem like ostentation, if we did not wait for the vacation which was now so near. If, before that date, I was to quit a public and conspicuous office, the attention of all men would

[1] Ps. cxx.   "The valley of tears " and "the climbing up," are from Ps. lxxxiii. 6, 7 of the Vulgate.

be drawn to my action; they would say that I
had been in a hurry to anticipate the day of the
vintage recess, because I wanted to give myself
importance.   And why should I desire that my
conversion should be the gossip of the town, and
that so my good should be evil spoken of?[1]
Further, that very summer my lungs had given
way under the stress of literary work; only with
difficulty could I draw a long breath; there were
pains in my chest that indicated mischief, and my
voice was husky and soon fatigued.   At first this
weakness had distressed me, because it seemed
likely to compel me either to lay down altogether
the load of my duties, or at anyrate to take a
rest, till I could undergo treatment and recover
my health.   But as soon as I formed a full and
firm resolve to be still and see that Thou art
God,[2] I began to rejoice (Thou knowest it, O
God) that I had here ready to hand a genuine
excuse, which would prevent the opposition of
the parents of my pupils, who for the sake of
their children would never have let me go free.

3. Full then of such joy I waited till the time
ran out.   Perhaps it was not so much as twenty
days, yet it was some strain upon my endurance,
for I had lost the ambition which used to lighten
the drudgery, and I should have been crushed
had not patience taken its place.   Some of Thy
servants, my brethren, may say that I sinned in
this, that, when my heart was fully bent upon
Thy service, I allowed myself to remain one
hour in the chair of falsehood.   Nor will I

[1] Rom. xiv. 16.   [2] Ps. xlvi. 10.

dispute it. But, O most merciful Lord, hast Thou not pardoned and forgiven this sin also, with all my other horrible and fatal misdoings, in Thy Holy Water?

CHAPTER III

Verecundus lends him his country house.

BUT this happiness of mine was a great trouble to Verecundus, because he saw that he was being deprived of my companionship, or rather that he had renounced my companionship, through the bonds which held him so fast. He was not yet a Christian, but his wife was, and she was in fact the heaviest of all the clogs upon him, and hindered him most effectually from the pilgrimage on which we had embarked. He said he did not care to be a Christian in any other way than that which for him was not possible. But he most kindly allowed us to occupy his country house so long as we stayed there. Thou wilt recompense him, O Lord, in the resurrection of the just,[1] for Thou hast already given unto him the lot of the righteous.[2] For, while I was absent at Rome, he was attacked by bodily sickness, became a faithful Christian, and so departed out of this life. So Thou didst deal mercifully not only with him but with me, saving me from the intolerable grief of remembering the great kindness of one, whom yet I could not reckon among Thy flock.

[1] Luke xiv. 14.   [2] Ps. cxxv. 3.

2. I thank Thee, O my God, for I am thine,
Thy warnings and Thy comforts prove it. Thy
promises are faithful. For that country house at
Cassicium, where we found shelter in Thee from
the storms of the world, Thou wilt repay to
Verecundus the delights of Thy paradise, where
spring is eternal—for Thou hast forgiven his sins
upon earth—on Thy mountain, Thy fruitful hill,
the mountain of milk and butter.[2] At that time
Verecundus felt sorrow, but Nebridius rejoiced with
me. For, although he also was not a Christian,
and had fallen into the pit of deadly error,
believing the flesh of Thy Son, the Truth, to be
an illusion, he had struggled forth and was his
own master once more; he was not yet dipped in
the sacraments of Thy church, yet he was an
eager enquirer after the truth. He too, not long
after my conversion and regeneration by Thy
baptism, became a faithful Catholic and served
Thee in Africa, his native land, in perfect chastity
and continence, with all his household whom he
had brought to Christ, till Thou didst set him
free from the flesh, and now he lives in Abraham's
bosom.[2]

3. Whatever that bosom signifies there lives
Nebridius, my own beloved friend, Thy freed-
man and adopted son, O Lord. Yes, there he
lives. For what other place is there for so

---

[1] *In monte incaseato*, the old Latin rendering of Ps.
lxviii. 15. The Vulgate (lxvii. 16) has *mons coagulatus*.
There is a play on *incaseato* and *Cassicium* which is hardly
translatable.

[2] Luke xvi. 22.

beautiful a soul? There he lives, in that abode
of which he used to ask me so many questions,
poor ignorant that I was. No longer does he
apply his ear to my lips, but sets his spiritual lips
to Thy fountain, and drinks in wisdom to the
full measure of his powers and of his thirst, and
is happy for evermore. Nor can I think him so
intoxicated by that draught as to forget me; for
Thou dost remember me, O Lord, and Thou
art that draught. Thus then it was with me.
I kept up my friendship with Verecundus, striving
to appease his sorrow at my sudden conversion, and
exhorting him to such a profession as suited his
degree, that is to say, the married life; and I
waited for Nebridius to rejoin me, expecting him
from hour to hour, as the distance was so small.
And, lo, at length those days rolled by. Many
and long did they seem in my yearning for peace
and freedom, that I might fall to singing from
my inmost parts, "My heart hath said unto
Thee, I have sought Thy Face. Thy Face,
Lord, will I seek.[1]

[1] Ps. **xxvii. 8**

CHAPTER IV

*Of the Books he wrote at Cassicium ; of his Letters
to Nebridius ; of the joy with which he read
the Psalms, and of his deliverance from
Toothache.*

SO the day came when I was formally set free
from my rhetoric professorship, from which
I was already released in mind. It was done.
Thou didst deliver my tongue, as Thou hadst
already delivered my heart, and I blessed Thee
with great joy, and returned to the country house.
What I wrote there, in a style which, though
already enlisted in Thy service, still breathed, in
that time of waiting, the pride of the school, is
on record in my *Discussions*, debates held with
such friends as were there, or with myself in
Thy sight, and in my *Letters* to Nebridius, who
was still away. How can I find time to relate
all Thy great goodness to me at that time, seeing
that I must hurry on to greater goodness still.
For my memory recalls, and sweet it is, O Lord,
to make the confession in Thy sight, by what
inward spurs Thou didst break me in, how
Thou didst make me like a level plain, bringing
low the mountains and hills of my thoughts,
making my crooked places straight and my
rough places smooth,[1] how Thou didst bring
Alypius, the brother of my heart, into sub-

[1] Is. xl. 4.

jection to the Name of Thy Only-begotten,
our Lord and Saviour Jesus Christ. This at
first he would not allow me to write, thinking
in his humility that my pages ought to smell
rather of the cedars of the Schools, which the
Lord hath broken,[1] than of those healing herbs
of the Church which are the serpent's bane.

2. O my God, how did I cry unto Thee, as
I read the Psalms of David, those hymns of
faith, whose pious accents leave no room for the
spirit of pride. I was still a beginner in Thy
true love, a catechumen keeping holiday in a
country place with Alypius, a catechumen like
myself, and my mother, a woman, yet in faith so
manly; hers were the tranquillity of age, the
love of a mother, the devotion of a true Christian.
How did I cry unto Thee in those Psalms!
how did they kindle my heart towards Thee!
how did I burn to sing them all over the world,
if so I might abate the haughtiness of the race
of man! Yet they are sung all over the world,
and there is none who can hide himself
from Thy sunshine.[2] What strong and poignant
indignation did I feel against the Manichees!
Yet, again, I could not but pity them, because
they knew not Thy healing sacraments, and
raved against the medicine that might have
cured them. Would that they could have
been somewhere near without my knowledge,
and looked upon my face, and learned from my

[1] Ps. xxix. 5.　　　　[2] Ps. xix. 6.

ejaculations, as I read the fourth [1] Psalm, what that Psalm had done for me!

3. "When I called, the God of my righteousness heard me; Thou didst enlarge me, when I was in distress. Have mercy upon me, O Lord, and hear my prayer." Would they could have heard without my knowing that they heard, lest they should have thought that I was speaking on their account, what I cried as I read these words! For indeed I could not so have cried, if I had felt that they were watching, nor, if I had used the very same expressions, would they have meant to them what they meant to me, as they poured from my heart in that soliloquy which Thou alone didst overhear. For I trembled with fear, and I glowed with hope and with great joy in Thy mercy, O my Father; all these emotions shone in my eyes and thrilled in my voice, while Thy good Spirit turned to us and said, "O ye sons of men, how long will ye be slow of heart? why do ye love vanity and seek after leasing?" For I had loved vanity and sought after leasing, and Thou, O Lord, hadst already magnified Thy Holy One, raising Him from the dead, and setting Him at Thy right hand, that thence He might send forth from on high His promise, the Paraclete, the Spirit of Truth. Already He had sent Him, and I knew it not.

4. He had sent Him, because he was already magnified, rising from the dead and ascending

[1] The Fourth Psalm, which St Augustine dwells upon here, should be read in the Vulgate.

into heaven. For, till then, the Spirit was not yet
given, because Jesus was not yet glorified. And
the prophet cries, " How long will ye be slow
of heart ? why do ye love vanity and seek after
leasing ? And know this, that the Lord hath
magnified His Holy One." He cries " How
long ?" he cries " Know this," and for all those
years I had not known, but loved vanity and
sought after leasing. Therefore I heard and
trembled : because the word is spoken to such
men as I remembered well that I had been.
In those phantasms, which I had held as truth,
there was vanity, there was leasing. And in the
sorrow of that recollection I pronounced aloud
my own stern and strong condemnation. Would
they could have heard me, who still love vanity
and seek after leasing ! Perchance they would
have been terrified, and have spued forth their
error, and Thou mightest have heard them
when they cried unto Thee. For it was by a
real death that He died for us, who now maketh
intercession for us before Thee.

5. I read, " Be ye angry and sin not." [1]
And how deeply was I touched, O my God, for
I had now learned to be angry with myself for
the past, that I might no more sin in the future.
Yes, and rightly to be angry ; for it was not
another nature belonging to the realm of darkness
which sinned in me, as they pretend who are
not angry with themselves, but treasure up unto
themselves wrath against the day of wrath and
revelation of Thy righteous judgment. Nor

[1] Ps. iv. 5 (Vulgate), *Irascimini et nolite peccare.*

were the good things I sought for any longer outside me, nor did I look for them with eyes of flesh in the light of this earthly sun; for they who desire joys from outside soon wither and are wasted away upon the things which are seen and temporal; yea, with their famished imaginations they lick even the dry bones. O that they might grow tired of hunger and say, "Who will shew us any good?" Then they would listen when we answered, "The light of Thy countenance is sealed upon us, O Lord." [1] For we are not the light that lighteth every man, [2] but Thou makest Thy light to shine upon us, so that we who were sometimes darkness are light in Thee. [3]

6. O that they could have seen the inner Light eternal which I had tasted, and gnashed my teeth because I could not shew it to them! O that they could only have come to me with their heart in their eyes, those wandering eyes, and said to me, "Who will shew us any good?" For there, in the inner chamber of my soul, where I was angry with myself, where I was filled with compunction, where I had offered sacrifice, slaying my old man and hoping in Thee with the nascent insight of a new life, even there Thou hadst become sweet unto me, and hadst put gladness into my heart. And I cried aloud, reading these things in the letter and recognising them in the spirit. Nor did I wish to be increased in earthly goods, wasting the gifts of

---

[1] Ps. iv. 7 (Vulgate), *Signatum est super nos lumen vultus tui Domine.*

[2] John i. 9.   [3] Eph. v. 8.

time and wasted by time, since in Thy eternal Oneness I possessed other corn and wine and oil.

7. And I cried aloud from the depth of my heart, as I read the following verse—"O, in peace; O, looking towards the Same [1] (Ah, see what he says), I will lay me down and take my rest." For who shall withstand us, when the saying that is written is brought to pass, "Death is swallowed up in victory." [2]   And surely Thou, who changest not, art that Same, and in Thee is rest and forgetfulness of all sorrow, since there is none other beside Thee, nor are we to toil for those many things, which are not Thou, for "Thou, Lord, only hast made me dwell in hope." I read with soul on fire; nor yet could I think how to help those deaf corpses, of whom I myself had been one.   Taught by these words of David I could see that I had been a bitter and blind reviler against a scripture honeyed with the honey of heaven, and luminous with Thy light; and I grieved over those who were still its adversaries.

8. When shall I recall the whole history of that time of holiday ? Nay, I have not forgotten it ; nor will I omit to tell of the sharpness of Thy scourge, the marvellous swiftness of Thy pity.   At that time Thou didst rack me with toothache, and, when the pain was so intense that I could not speak, the thought came into my

[1] Ps. iv. 9 (Vulgate), *in pace in idipsum dormiam.* The word *idipsum* St Augustine took as denoting the Sameness and Eternity of God.

[2] 1 Cor. xv. 54.

heart to call upon my friends to pray for me to Thee, the God of all health. So I wrote this on my tablets, and gave it them to read. So soon as we bowed our knees in supplication the pain was gone. What was that pain, and how did it go? I trembled, O Lord God, my God; I confess it; for never from my birth had the same thing befallen me. Thus in the deep was Thy guidance revealed unto me, and rejoicing in faith I praised Thy Name. But that faith suffered me not to be at rest concerning my former sins, which had not yet been forgiven me through Thy Baptism.

CHAPTER V.

He asks Ambrose for guidance in his reading.

AS soon as the vintage recess was over, I sent word to the Milanese that they must find another dealer in words for their students, because I had determined to serve Thee, and because I was no longer fit for the Professorship of Rhetoric, owing to my difficulty in breathing and the pain in my chest. And by letter I intimated to the holy Ambrose, Thy bishop, my former errors and my present resolve, begging him to advise me which of Thy books I should chiefly read to fit and prepare myself for the reception of so great a grace. He bade me study the prophet Isaiah, I presume because

Isaiah is the clearest foreteller of the Gospel and of the calling of the Gentiles. But I could not understand the first chapter that I read, and, thinking that the whole would be equally difficult, laid the book aside to be resumed when I had more practice in the divine style.

CHAPTER VI.

He is Baptized at Milan with Alypius and Adeodatus.

WHEN the time came for giving in my name, we left the country and returned to Milan. Alypius also resolved to be born again in Thee at the same time; he was already endued with the humility that befits Thy sacraments, and so sturdily did he discipline his flesh that he would walk barefoot on the frozen Italian soil, a feat that few dare venture. We joined with ourselves the boy Adeodatus, my son after the flesh, the off-spring of my sin. Thou hadst made him nobly. He was but fifteen, yet in ability surpassed many grave and learned men. I confess unto Thee Thy gifts, O Lord my God, Creator of all, who art abundantly able to reshape all our unshapeliness: for I had no share in that boy except the sin. Truly I had schooled him in Thy good breeding, but by Thy inspiration and Thine alone. I confess unto Thee Thy gifts. There is a book of mine called "*the Master*;" it is a dialogue be-

tween him and myself. Thou knowest that all
the thoughts, which are there put into the mouth
of my interlocutor, are his, though he was then
but sixteen. Much more, and yet more marvellous, did I find in him. His intelligence filled
me with awe; for who but Thou can work such
miracles?

2. Early didst Thou cut off his life from the
earth; and I remember him without a shadow of
misgiving, for I fear nothing for his boyhood or
his youth or any fraction of his existence. We
took him for our companion, as of the same age
in grace with ourselves, to be trained with ourselves in Thy schooling, and so we were baptized,
and all anxiety for the past fled away. Nor
could I be satisfied during these days with the
surpassing joy of musing upon the depths of Thy
wisdom in the salvation of the human race.
What tears did I shed over the hymns and can-
ticles, when the sweet sound of the music of Thy
Church thrilled my soul! As the music flowed
into my ears, and Thy truth trickled into my
heart, the tide of devotion swelled high within
me, and the tears ran down, and there was gladness in those tears.

CHAPTER VII.

Of the institution of Hymn Singing at Milan, and of the discovery of the bodies of Gervasius and Protasius.

THE church of Milan had but recently begun to practise this kind of consolation and exhortation, to the great delight of the brethren who sang together with heart and voice. It was about a year from the time when Justina, mother of the boy Emperor Valentinian, entered upon her persecution of Thy holy man Ambrose, because he resisted the heresy into which she had been seduced by the Arians. The people of God were keeping ward in the church ready to die with Thy servant, their bishop. Among them was my mother, living unto prayer, and bearing a chief part in that anxious watch. Even I myself, though as yet untouched by the fire of Thy spirit, shared in the general alarm and distraction. Then it was that the custom arose of singing hymns and psalms, after the use of the Eastern provinces, to save the people from being utterly worn out by their long and sorrowful vigils. From that day to this it has been retained, and many, I might say all Thy flocks, throughout the rest of the world now follow our example.

2. At that time Thou didst reveal in a vision to Thy famous Bishop the unknown grave of Thy martyrs, Gervasius and Protasius, whose bodies

Thou hadst preserved incorrupt for so many
years in Thy secret treasury, that Thou mightest
bring them forth in due time to check the fury
of one who was a woman indeed but yet a queen.
They were discovered and disinterred, and translated with fitting state to the basilica of Ambrose.
And, as they were borne along the road, many
who were tormented by unclean spirits were
healed, the very devils being constrained to make
confession.   Nay, there was one, a citizen, and
well known to have been blind for many years,
who, when he learned the reason of that loud
rejoicing, leaped up and begged his guide to lead
him to the spot.   It was done, and on his earnest
entreaty he was allowed to touch with his hand-
kerchief the bier of Thy saints, whose death is
so precious in Thy sight.[1]   He laid the kerchief
on his eyes, and immediately they were opened.
Hence wonder ran abroad ; hence Thy glory
shone more bright ; hence that she-oppressor,
though not humbled to the wisdom of belief, was
yet restrained from the madness of persecution.
Thanks be to Thee, O my God.   Whence and
whither hast Thou guided my memory, that I
should confess unto Thee these great mercies
also, which I had forgotten and passed by?
And yet at that time, when the sweet savour of
Thy ointments was so fragrant, I did not run
after Thee.   And therefore did I weep the more
bitterly as I listened to Thy hymns.   Long had
I panted after Thee, and now at length I could
breathe Thee, as one who breathes the air in a
hut of straw.

[1] Ps. cxvi. 5.

CHAPTER VIII

*The confession of Evodius.   The death of his
Mother and her early education.*

THOU that makest men to be of one mind in
a house [1] didst join to us Evodius also, a
young man of my own township.   He had been
a clerk in the Home Office,[2] was converted
before me and baptized, and renounced a worldly
service to enlist in Thine.   We lived in company, and purposed still to dwell together in the
holy life which we had chosen. We were considering in what place we could serve Thee most
profitably, and were on our way back to Africa.
But when we had reached Ostia, the port of
Tiber, my mother died.   Much I omit by reason
of my haste.   Accept my confession and my
thanks, O my God, for countless mercies which
I leave untold.   But I must not omit to tell
what my soul yearns to bring to birth concerning
her, Thy handmaid, who brought me to birth,
her who was twice my mother, in the flesh that
I might be born into this earthly light, in heart
that I might be born into light eternal.   Yet
what I shall record is not her grace, but Thy
grace in her.   She did not create herself, nor did
she train herself.

   2. Thou didst create her; nor did father or

---

[1] Ps. lxviii. 6.
[2] *Agens in Rebus.*   See above viii. 6. 5.

mother know what their daughter should be.
And the rod of Thy Christ, the rule of Thy
Only Son, educated her in Thy fear, in a faithful household, in a living branch of Thy Church.
Yet, as she told me, she owed her training not
so much to the care of her mother, as to a
decrepit old maid-servant who had nursed her
father, carrying him upon her back, as big girls
carry babies. For the sake of this service, for
her age also and excellent character, she was
treated with much respect by her master and mistress in that Christian household. Hence the
charge of the daughters of the family had been
entrusted to her. This duty she faithfully performed, using discipline when necessary, with
strict and holy severity, and instructing with great
sense and prudence. For except at the appointed
hours, when they took their temperate meals at
their parents' board, she would not suffer them
to drink even water, no, not though they were
parched with thirst, so fearful was she of the
formation of a bad habit. " Now," she would
say, adding a wise word of advice, " now you
drink water, because you cannot get wine. When
you are married, and have the keys of cupboards
and cellars, you will not care for water, but the
habit of drinking will be fixed."

By such precepts and such use of her authority
she curbed the greediness of their unreflecting
age, and taught the girls to regulate even their
thirst by the standard of virtue, so that they
no longer cared to do what was not becoming.
And yet, as Thy handmaid told me, her son, the

love of wine had stolen upon my mother. For
when in the usual way her parents sent her, as a
sober maiden, to draw wine from the cask, she
would hold the cup under the tap, and then, before
she poured the liquor into the flagon, just touch
the brim with her lips and swallow a few drops,
for at first she disliked the taste. Nor did she do
this from any love of the excitement produced
by wine, but merely from that freakish impulse
of childhood, which bubbles up in all kinds of
playful tricks, and is generally repressed by the
authority of elders.

4. And so, adding daily a little to that little
(for " he that contemneth small things shall fall by
little and little " [1]), she slipped into such a habit
that she would drink greedily one cup after
another, almost full of strong wine. Where now
was that wise old woman and her strict prohibi-
tion ? Can aught avail against the lurking disease,
unless Thy healing power, O Lord, keeps watch
over us ? Father, mother, teacher were absent ;
but thou wast present, who didst create, who
dost call, who, even by the agency of bad men,
dost work for the salvation of our souls. How
didst Thou work for her, O my God ? how
didst Thou treat and cure her ? Didst Thou
not bring forth from another soul a hard and
biting taunt, drawing, as it were, a surgeon's
knife from Thy secret resources, and with one
stroke cut off that festering tumour.

5. For a slave-girl, who used to go to the
cellar with her, fell to scolding with her young

[1] Ecclesiasticus xix. 1.

mistress when they were alone, as sometimes happens, and reproached her with this fault, calling her in bitter insult "a drunkard." The dart went home; she saw her own vileness, and straightway condemned and renounced it. As the flattery of friends corrupts, so often do the taunts of enemies instruct. Yet dost Thou repay them, not the good Thou workest by their means, but the malice they intended. That angry slave-girl wanted to infuriate her little mistress, not to correct her, and that is why she spoke when they were alone; or perhaps it was because their quarrel happened to break out at that time and place; or perhaps again she was afraid of punishment for not having told before. And Thou, O Lord, Ruler of heaven and earth, who makest the rage of the waterfloods to serve Thy will, and swayest the wild tide of the centuries, Thou didst order the sin of one soul to heal the sin of another. Let no man, then, who hears this tale, ascribe it to his own power, if one, whom he wishes to convert, is converted by his word.

CHAPTER IX

He enlarges upon the excellent virtues of his Mother.

THUS chastely and soberly brought up, made subject by Thee to her parents rather than by her parents to Thee, as soon as her years were

ripe for marriage, she was given to a husband,
and served him as her lord, labouring to gain
him unto Thee, preaching Thee to him by that
character whereby Thou hadst made her beautiful,
dutifully amiable, and altogether admirable in her
husband's sight.   She endured with patience his
infidelities, and never had any disagreement with
her husband for this cause.   For she looked for
Thy mercy towards him, that he might believe
in Thee and so be made pure.   He was a man,
moreover, of great good-humour, but of violent
temper.   She had learned not to resist the anger
of her husband by deed or word.   But, when
he was composed and quieted, and she found
her opportunity, she would explain her conduct,
if it so happened that he had taken groundless
offence.

2. In fine, when matrons, whose husbands
were not so passionate as hers, came and talked
to her, showing the bruises on their faces and
complaining of their husband's lives, she would
playfully but seriously blame their tongues, telling them that, when once they had heard the
marriage lines read over to them, they ought to
have looked upon them as indentures by which
they were made handmaids; they ought therefore
to remember their condition, and not rebel against
their lords and masters.   And, when they wondered at such words, knowing what a fiery
husband she had to put up with, yet knowing
also that no one had ever heard, nor seen any
mark to prove, that Patricius had beaten his wife,
or been estranged from her for one single day by

any domestic quarrel, if they asked the reason, she told them her rule of conduct, which I have explained above. Those who followed her advice had good cause to be thankful; those who rejected it were trampled upon and illused.

3. Her mother-in-law also, who at first was set against her by the whisperings of mischief-making servants, she so won upon by persevering attentions and forbearance and gentleness, that of her own accord she complained to her son of the meddlesome tongues, by which the family peace had been disturbed, and requested him to punish them. And when he, in compliance with his mother's desire, and for the good order of his family and the harmony of its members, had chastised those whom she pointed out to him with as many stripes as she judged sufficient, she gave notice that anyone, who should in future think to give her pleasure by speaking ill of her daughter-in-law, might expect the same reward. Henceforth no one dared to sow discord, and the two ladies lived together in perfect goodwill and agreement. Another great gift also didst Thou bestow on that good servant, in whose womb Thou didst form me O God, my Mercy, that, whenever she could, she acted the part of peacemaker between divided and discordant souls, and never repeated to the one the bitter things which she had heard from the other—those outbreaks of undigested spleen which hatred spits forth behind its enemy's back in sour speeches to a friendly ear—unless, by so doing, she could promote a reconciliation.

4. This would seem to me but a small virtue, did I not know to my sorrow a host of people (so widely does the horrid infection of sin diffuse itself) who not only repeat the words of angry men to angry men, but add to them what was never said at all. Now surely a man of humane spirit ought not merely to abstain from arousing or exasperating a quarrel by evil words—this is a little thing— but to do his utmost to allay it by kindly words. Such was my mother's way, learned from Thee in the school of the heart, where Thou wast Master. Lastly, she gained unto Thee her own husband, towards the very end of his earthly life, nor after his conversion had she ever again to lament those faults which she had endured in the days of his unbelief.

5. Moreover, she was the servant of Thy servants. All who knew her, praised, honoured, loved Thee in her, because she felt Thy presence in her heart, whereof the fruits of her holy conversation were the proof. She had been the wife of one husband, she had requited her parents, had governed her house piously, was well reported of for good works, had brought up children,[1] of whom she travailed in birth [2] anew, as often as she saw them go astray from Thee. Lastly, O Lord, since of Thy bounty Thou sufferest us to speak, she tended like a mother, she served like a daughter all of us Thy servants, who, before she fell asleep, had received the grace of baptism and were living in companionship in Thee.

[1] 1 Tim. v. 4, *seq.*   [2] Gal. iv. 19.

CHAPTER X.

His conversation with his Mother on the kingdom of heaven.

AS the day drew near on which she was to depart from this life; Thou knewest it though we did not; it fell out, as I believe, through the secret workings of Thy providence, that she and I were leaning by ourselves on the ledge of a window, from which we looked down on the garden of our house. Yonder it was, in Ostia by Tiber, where, away from the crowd, fatigued by the long journey from Milan, we were recruiting ourselves for the sea voyage. Sweet was the converse we held together, as, forgetting those things which were behind, and reaching forth unto those things which were before,[1] we asked ourselves in the presence of Thee, the Truth, what will be the manner of that eternal life of the saints, which eye hath not seen, nor ear heard, neither hath it entered into the heart of man.[2] With the lips of our souls we panted for the heavenly streams of Thy fountain, the fountain of life which is with Thee, that, sprinkled with that water to the measure of our capacity, we might attain some poor conception of that glorious theme.

2. And as our converse drew to this conclusion, that the sweetest conceivable delight of

[1] Phil. iii. 13.   [2] 1 Cor. ii. 9.

sense in the brightest conceivable earthly sunshine
was not to be compared, no, nor even named,
with the happiness of that life, we soared with
glowing hearts towards the Same, mounting step
by step the ladder of the material order, through
heaven itself, whence sun and moon and stars
shed their radiance upon earth.   And still
higher did we climb by the staircase of the
spirit, thinking and speaking of Thee, and
marvelling at Thy works.   And so we came
to our own minds, and passed beyond them
into the region of unfailing plenty, where Thou
feedest Israel for ever with the food of truth,
where Life is Wisdom by which all these things
come to be, both the things that have been and
the things that shall be; and the Life itself
never comes to be, but is, as it was and shall
be evermore, because in it is neither past nor
future but present only, for it is eternal; for past
and future are not eternal.   And as we talked
and yearned after it, we touched it for an instant
with the whole force of our hearts.   And we
sighed, and left there impawned the first fruits of
the spirit,[1] and heard again the babble of our own
tongues, wherein each word has a beginning and
an ending.   Far unlike Thy Word, our Lord,
who abideth in Himself, never growing old and
making all things new.

3. We said then:[2] "If the tumult of the

[1] Rom. viii. 23.
[2] Here again the thought and even the expressions
of St Augustine seem to be suggested by Plotinus.
See *Ennead*, v. 1, 2

x

flesh were hushed; hushed these shadows of earth, sea, sky; hushed the heavens and the soul itself, so that it should pass beyond itself and not think of itself; if all dreams were hushed, and all sensuous revelations, and every tongue and every symbol; if all that comes and goes were hushed—They all proclaim to him that hath an ear: 'We made not ourselves: He made us who abideth for ever'—But suppose that, having delivered their message, they held their peace, turning their ear to Him who made them, and that He alone spoke, not by them but for Himself, and that we heard His word, not by any fleshly tongue, nor by an angel's voice, nor in the thunder, nor in any similitude, but His voice whom we love in these His creatures—Suppose we heard Him without any intermediary at all— Just now we reached out, and with one flash of thought touched the Eternal Wisdom that abides above all—Suppose this endured, and all other far inferior modes of vision were taken away, and this alone were to ravish the beholder, and absorb him, and plunge him in mystic joy, might not eternal life be like this moment of comprehension for which we sighed? Is not this the meaning of 'Enter thou into the joy of thy Lord?'[1] Ah, when shall this be? Shall it be when 'we shall all rise, but shall not all be changed'?"[2]

4. Thus we spoke; not perhaps in this fashion or in these precise words; but Thou knowest,

---

[1] Matt. xxv. 21.

[2] I Cor. xv 51, agreeing with the Vulgate.

O Lord, that as we thus talked on that day this
world with all its delights seemed but a poor
thing. Then said my mother: "My son, as
for me, I find no further pleasure in life. What
I am still to do, or why I still linger here, I
know not, for the hope of this world is dead
within me. There was but one object, for
which I desired to tarry a little longer in this
life, that I might see thee a Catholic Christian
before I died. My God has granted me this
boon in full measure and running over; I see
thee His servant, and caring not for earthly
happiness. What do I here?"

CHAPTER XI

Of the Ecstasy and Death of his Mother.

WHAT answer I made to her, I hardly
remember. Within five days, or a little
more, she was seized by a fever, and during this
sickness fell into a swoon, and lost for awhile
all consciousness. We ran to her aid, but she
soon recovered her senses, and seeing my brother [1]

---

[1] Monnica had more sons than one (ix. 9, 4, *nutrierat
filios*), and Augustine is known to have had nieces. The
brother is that Navigius whom St Augustine calls
frater meus in *de Beata Vita* i. 6. He seems to have been
delicate in health, and took part in the philosophical
conversation on Augustine's "birthday." Possidius in

and myself standing by the bed asked us, "Where
was I?" Then, as we could not speak for grief,
she fixed her eyes upon us and said, "Here you
will bury your mother." I held my peace,
keeping back my tears ; my brother spoke something to the effect that he trusted she would die
not abroad, but in her own native land, as thinking this a happier lot. When she heard this, she
cast upon him a look of reproach for cherishing
such fancies, and then turning to me said, "See
how he talks." Then to both of us she added,
"Lay this body where you will, and be not
anxious about it. Only I beseech you, remember me at the altar of God, wherever you
are."

2. When she had delivered this injunction, in
such words as she could muster, she said no more,
and fell into an agony. But I, pondering on the
graces, O Thou invisible God, which Thou dost
infuse into the hearts of Thy faithful ones, whence
such marvellous fruits do grow, was filled with
joy and gave thanks unto Thee. For well I
knew how solicitous she had always been about
the grave which she had provided and prepared
for herself beside the body of her husband. For,
because they had lived together in great harmony,
she craved for yet another happiness, that all men
should know that she had been permitted to
return from her wanderings beyond sea, and

the *Life*, c. 26, mentions the *fratris filiae*. See Tille-
mont xiii. 3. It is curious that the brother should be
so abruptly introduced here, without name and without
previous mention.

mingle her dust with her husband's. So little can the human soul understand the purposes of God.

3. At what time this fond desire had begun, in the plenitude of Thy goodness, to die away within her I knew not, and I felt both joy and wonder that so it should be. And yet from the words which she had spoken, when we were leaning upon the window, "What do I here," it was evident that she had no longing to die at home. Afterwards I heard that, shortly after our arrival at Ostia, when I was not present, she spoke with a mother's frankness to some of my friends on the contempt of this life and the blessedness of death. They were amazed at the courage which Thou hadst given to her, a weak woman, and asked whether she did not shrink from the thought of leaving her body so far from her own home. She replied, "Nothing is far to God. There is no fear that at the end of the world He will not know whence to summon me." And so on the ninth day of her sickness, in the fifty-sixth year of her age, and the thirty-third of mine, that devout and godly soul was released from the body.

CHAPTER XII

How he mourned the Death of his Mother.

I CLOSED her eyes, and a great tide of sorrow surged into my heart and would have run over in weeping. Yet my eyes by a strong effort of will drove back the tears even unto dryness, and in that struggle it went very hard with me. As she drove her last breath, the boy Adeodatus broke out into lamentations; but we all rebuked him, and he was silent again. So the childish nature within me, which would have melted in tears, was rebuked by the manly voice of my heart, and held its peace. For we judged it not seemly that such a death should be attended by weeping, and those cries of grief wherewith the world bewails what it counts the misery or utter extinction of the departed. She was not miserable nor was she wholly dead. This we knew for certain from the life she had led, from faith unfeigned, from reasons which we could not doubt.

2. What then was that aching pain in my heart? What but the bleeding wound, caused by the sudden tearing away of that sweet and precious intercourse? I treasured up her praise, for in her last illness, when I was rendering her some little service, she caressed me, and called me "her good son," and said with great emotion that she had never heard from my lips an angry

or disrespectful word. But yet, O my God and Creator, what comparison can there be between my respect for my mother and my mother's drudgery for me? And so, because I was bereft of that precious solace, my soul was wounded, and my life was rent in twain, for her life and mine had been but one.

3. And so, when the weeping of the boy was stilled, Evodius caught up a psalter, and began to chant the psalm, " My song shall be of mercy and judgment; unto Thee, O Lord, will I sing," [1] and the whole household took up the response. As the news spread many brethren and religious women came together; and, while they, whose duty it was, made arrangements for the funeral, I retired into another chamber and spoke to those who thought proper to attend me such words as fitted the occasion. So the balsam of truth soothed the anguish which was known to Thee. They knew it not, but listened intently and imagined that I had no sense of grief. But in Thy hearing, where none of them could hear, I was chiding the softness of my heart, and holding back the tide of sorrow. It ebbed a little, and then surged up again, as is its nature, yet not so that I should drop a tear, or change my countenance; but well did I know what I was choking down in my heart. And because I was greatly distressed that these accidents of our humanity, which must needs befal us, through the law and lot of our earthly state, should have such power over me, I grieved for my grief with a

[1] Ps. ci. 1.

second grief, and was wasting with a double sorrow, when, lo, the corpse was carried to the burial.

4. We went and returned without a tear. Not even at those prayers which we poured forth unto Thee, when the body rests beside the tomb, before it is committed to the ground, and the sacrifice of our Redemption is offered for the departed, as is the custom there—not even at those prayers did I weep. But all that day I sorrowed in secret, and with troubled mind besought Thee, as best I could, to heal my grief. But Thou wouldest not hear, because Thou wouldest have me remember, as I believe, by this one instance, the power of habit even over a soul which feeds upon no deceiving words. I determined even to go and bathe; for I had heard that the bath derives its name from the Greek word βαλανεῖον, because it drives away sorrow from the mind. Behold, this also I confess to Thy mercy, O Father of the fatherless,[1] that I went and bathed, and was the same after the bath as before! For the bitterness of my trouble could not be washed away from my heart.

5. Then I slept and woke, and found my sorrow diminished not a little. And as I lay alone upon my bed, I recalled the truthful verses of Thy servant Ambrose. For indeed Thou art

" Creator of the earth and sky,[2]
Ruling the firmament on high,

[1] Ps. lxviii. 5.
[2] The whole of the Ambrosian hymn, *Deus Creator Omnium*, is extant. It may be found in the Sarum Breviary.

Clothing the day with robes of light,
Blessing with gracious sleep the night,

That rest may comfort weary men,
And brace to useful toil again,
And soothe awhile the harassed mind,
And sorrow's heavy load unbind "

Thus little by little I came back to my former thoughts of Thy handmaid and her life, so devoted to Thee, so kind and complaisant, in all that befits a saint, towards us. And as I dwelt upon that sudden loss, I wept freely in Thy sight over her and for her, over myself and for myself. I gave my pent up tears license to flow as they would, and laid them as a bed for my heart. And it found rest upon them; for Thy ears alone could hear my weeping, not man, who might have scorned me.

6. And now, O Lord, I confess it unto Thee in my book. Let anyone that will read it, and make of it what he will. And if he count it a sin that for a fraction of an hour I should have wept for my mother, that mother who in my sight for a while was dead, who had wept so many years for me that I might live in Thy sight, yet let him not scoff at me; but rather, if his charity be large, let him weep for my sins unto Thee, the Father of all the brethren of Thy Christ.

CHAPTER XIII

He prays for his Dead Mother.

FROM that time, my heart being healed of that wound, in which some might discover the fault of carnal affection, I have poured forth unto Thee, O my God, a very different kind of tears for that handmaid of Thine, the tears which flow from a spirit shaken to its depth by the thought of the peril that awaits every soul that dieth in Adam.[1] Although she had been made alive in Christ, and, even before her deliverance from the flesh, lived so that Thy name was glorified in her faith and conversation, yet I dare not affirm that, from the day of her regeneration in baptism, no word had passed her lips contrary to Thy commandments. And the Truth, Thy Son, hath said, "Whosoever shall say unto his brother, Thou fool, shall be in danger of hell fire."[2] Woe even unto them whose life is praiseworthy, if Thou shouldest weigh it without pity! Because Thou art not extreme to mark what is done amiss,[3] we have a good hope to find some place of indulgence in Thy sight. And yet if a man counts up unto Thee his real merits, what does he count up but so many gifts of Thine? O that all men might

[1] 1 Cor. xv. 22.   [2] Matt. v. 22.
[3] Ps. cxxx. 3.

know themselves! that he who glorieth might glory in the Lord![1]

2. I therefore, O my Glory and my Life, Thou God of my heart, putting aside for a time those good deeds of my mother for which I joyfully thank Thee, do now entreat Thee for her sins. By that Medicine of our wounds, who hung upon the tree, and now sitteth at Thy right hand to make intercession for us,[2] O hear me. I know that she dealt mercifully, and forgave from her heart the debts of her debtors. Do Thou forgive her the debts[3] that she may have incurred in a life of many years, since the time when she entered the water of salvation. Forgive them, O Lord, forgive them, I beseech Thee: enter not into judgment with her.[4] Let mercy rejoice against judgment,[5] for Thy words are true, and Thou hast promised mercy unto the merciful.[6] That they were so was Thy gift, who wilt have mercy on whom Thou wilt have mercy, and wilt have compassion on whom Thou wilt have compassion.[7] And, as I do believe, Thou hast already performed what I entreat for; yet do Thou accept, O Lord, the freewill offerings of my mouth.[8]

3. For, when the day of Thy purpose came upon her, she cared not that her body should be richly shrouded, or wrapped in spices; she desired no proud monument, nor prayed for a

[1] 2 Cor. x. 17.   [2] Rom. viii. 34.
[3] Matt. xviii. 35.   [4] Ps. cxliii. 2.
[5] James ii. 13.   [6] Matt. v. 7.
[7] Rom. ix. 15.   [8] Ps. cxix. 108.

grave in her native land. Not such were her last injunctions to us, but only she begged that we would remember her before Thy altar, which she had served without missing a day, whence, as she knew, is dispensed that Holy Victim, whereby the handwriting that was against us is blotted out,[1] wherein the enemy that reckons up our sins, and seeketh for accusations against us, and could find nothing in Him[2] in whom we conquer, is trodden under foot. Who shall repay to Him the innocent blood? Who shall give Him back the price wherewith He bought us, that he should pluck us out of His hand? With that Sacrament of our Redemption Thy handmaiden bound up her soul with the bond of faith.

4. Let none have power to drag her away from Thy protection. Let not the lion nor the dragon[3] bar her path by force or by fraud. For she will not answer that she owes nothing, lest she should be confuted and seized by the crafty accuser; but she will answer that all her debt has been forgiven by Him, to whom none can give back the ransom which He paid on our behalf, though He owed it not. May she rest in peace, therefore, with her husband, her first and only husband, whom she obeyed, bringing forth fruit unto Thee with patience,[4] that she might gain him also unto Thee. And do Thou inspire, O Lord my God, do Thou inspire Thy servants, my brethren, Thy sons, my masters,

[1] Col. ii. 14.   [2] John xiv. 30.
[3] Ps. xci. 13.   [4] Luke viii. 15.

whom I serve with heart and voice and pen, that whoso reads these pages may remember before Thy altar Monnica, Thy handmaid, and Patricius, once her husband, through whose flesh Thou didst bring me into this life, I know not how. Let them remember with godly love those who were my parents in this transitory life, those who were my brethren under Thee, our Father, in the Catholic mother, those who are my fellow-citizens in the eternal Jerusalem, for which Thy people of pilgrims yearn from their going out until their coming home again. So shall her dying request be granted to her in richer abundance by the prayers of many, through my *Confessions* rather than through my prayers.

PRINTED BY
TURNBULL AND SPEARS
EDINBURGH